AN INTRODUCTION TO THE STUDY OF BALI NYONGA

Spears Studies in African and African Diaspora History

1. *Basel Mission Education in Cameroon: 1886–1968* by Mathew B. Gwanfogbe
2. *In Search of Harmony: A History of Bali Nyonga* by Fondi Ndifontah Nyamndi
3. *An Introduction to the Study of Bali Nyonga: A Tribute to His Royal Highness Galega II, Traditional Ruler of Bali Nyonga from 1940–1985* by Vincent Titanji, Mathew Gwanfogbe, Elias Nwana, Gwannua Ndangam, Adolf Sema Lima

AN INTRODUCTION TO THE STUDY OF BALI NYONGA

A Tribute to His Royal Highness Galega II, Traditional Ruler of Bali Nyonga from 1940–1985

Vincent Titanji
Mathew Gwanfogbe
Elias Nwana
Gwannua Ndangam
Adolf Sema Lima

Revised Edition
With a New Introduction
By Jude D. Fokwang

SPEARS BOOKS
Denver, Colorado

Spears Books
An Imprint of Spears Media Press LLC
21699 E Quincy Ave, Unit F #167
Aurora, CO 80015
United States of America

First published by Stardust Printers, B.P. 8361, Yaounde, Cameroon, 1988

Revised Edition Published in the United States of America in 2025 by Spears Books
www.spearsbooks.org
info@spearsmedia.com
Information on this title:
https://spearsbooks.org/product/an-introduction-to-the-study-of-bali-nyonga

ISBN: 9781957296692 (Paperback)
ISBN: 9781957296708 (eBook)

Designed and typeset by Spears Media Press LLC
Cover design: D. Kambem

Distributed globally by African Books Collective (ABC)
www.africanbookscollective.com

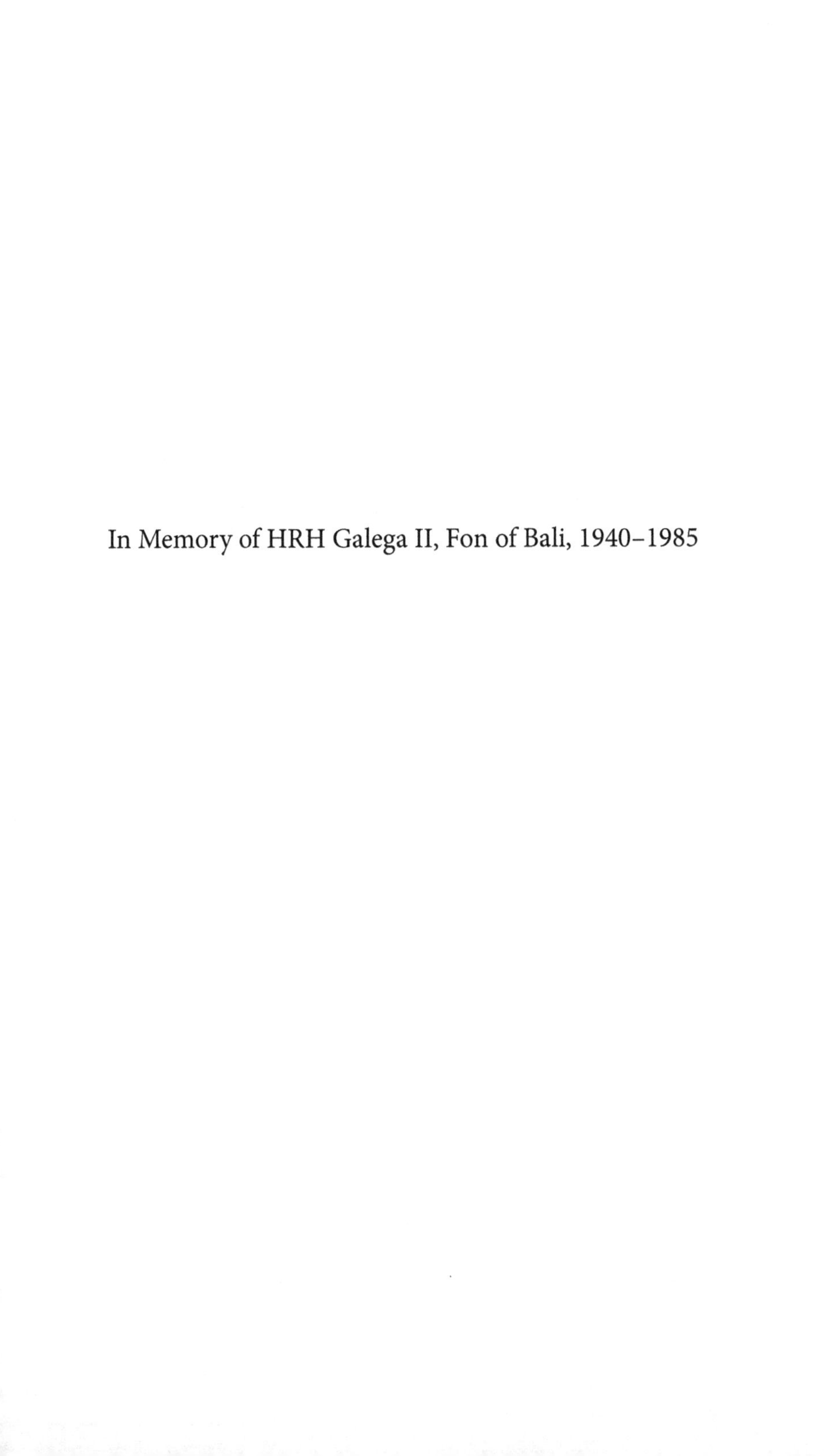

In Memory of HRH Galega II, Fon of Bali, 1940–1985

GALEGA I
FONYONGA II
GALEGA II
GANYONGA III

Contents

Figures

Foreword to the First Edition

The history and culture of the Bali Nyonga people has for long enjoyed an enviable position in the writings of scholars researching on the Western Grassfield. Among the factors to which this is attributable are, not only the dynamism of the people but also, and especially the quality of their leadership, as will be evidenced in this text.

Since the publication of *The Living Culture of the Bali Nyonga People* in 1979, the people have been increasingly aware of the need to document their history and culture for current use and for posterity. The present volume is a step in that direction; it also intends to rectify some of the many factual distortions of our history that have been conscious or inadvertent.

Above all, the authors have decided to pay tribute to their illustrious leader, whose prowess and insight brought unity as well as political, economic and social development in the region. Our late leader was distinguished by his charismatic and commanding character, coupled with his shrewdness and administrative knack which gained him undeniable recognition far beyond the limits of his territory.

While commending the initiative of this team, I wish to call on all Bali people and everyone interested in the Bali history and culture to read this richly informative work.

Bali, March 1988

Dr. D. Ganyonga, Fon of Bali

Preface to the First Edition

On 8th of September 1985 a major event took place in the recent history of Bali Nyonga, of North West Province of Cameroon. His Royal Highness V.S. Galega II, Fon of Bali from 1940–1985 died. Because of his personal contribution to the history of Bali, and the struggle for the independence and unification of Cameroon, we felt it appropriate to pay him tribute. This document which in no way pretends to exhaust the significance of his contributions is an expression of such a tribute. Naturally we took this opportunity to present at the same time an overall introduction to Bali Nyonga, which is important in this context not only as the home-base of V.S. Galega II, but also of interest for scholars of Western Grassfields of Cameroon.

We therefore set up as an objective to review a wide range of topics with particular emphasis on their evolution during the reign of V.S. Galega II. In the course of such an exercise we hoped to set the record right on a number of facts which have appeared in recent publications. Thus our approach consisted in presenting broad reviews of selected themes rather than in-depth analysis of a single subject. Chapter I of the study deals with a geographical and historical introduction of Bali Nyonga whereas Chapter II & III deal with the reign of Galega II. To give a perspective to the actions of V.S. Galega II, we present in Chapter IV a general description of the institutions that conferred traditional authority on him. Chapter V discusses the development of the Mungaka language. The work is completed by an appendix introducing His Royal Highness, Dr. Ganyonga

In preparing the manuscript we divided the topics to various authors who after the appropriate research exchanged drafts for comments and corrections. Thus the opinions expressed in each of the chapters are those of the authors.

We hope that this work would portray, at least in outline, the role of V.S. Galega II and in addition serve as a source for further studies. We would like to take this opportunity to thank all our informants for their help in making this work possible.

V. Titanji, M. Gwanfogbe, E. Nwana, A. Ndangam, A. Lima

24th March 1987
Bali Nyonga
North West Province

Introduction
V.S. Galega II and the Chroniclers of His Enduring Legacy

Jude D. Fokwang

V.S. Galega II ascended the throne of Bali Nyonga at the age of 34, becoming the first of a new generation of Western-educated kings in the region. He reigned for 45 years, emerging as one of the most influential Bali kings of the 20th century and leaving a lasting impact on the sociocultural and political life of not only his kingdom but also the entire Grasslands. His reign coincided with the emergence of an educated class that recognised the significance of documenting Bali culture, having witnessed or experienced it. Inspired by the legacy of colonial ethnographers from the late 19th century, who had capitalised on Bali's friendly relations with the German colonial project and later, British ethnographic reports, these Bali intellectuals began recording Bali history and culture in the 1970s, catalysing a trend that, today, has led to numerous monographs on Bali history, society and culture. It was therefore fitting that, upon Galega II's passing, some of these leading Bali voices gathered to reflect and pay tribute to a towering figure for his "personal contribution to the history of Bali, and the struggle for the independence and unification of Cameroon…" (Titanji et al., 1988, p. vii).

Between 1986 and 1988, Vincent Titanji, Mathew Gwanfogbe, Elias Nwana, Gwannua Ndangam and Adolf Lima diligently documented for posterity aspects of Bali culture as they had evolved during the reign of Galega II. Their efforts bore fruit when, in the spring of 1988, the multi-authored book, *An Introduction to the Study of Bali-Nyonga: A Tribute to His Royal Highness Galega II, Traditional Ruler of Bali-Nyonga from 1940–1985,* was published. Although its scope was intended to present "broad reviews of selected themes rather than in-depth analysis of a single subject" (Titanji et al., 1988, p. vii) and to serve as a source for further studies, the volume has progressively established its position in Bali scholarship as a pioneering and outstanding work. It would take almost three decades for another project of this magnitude to emerge with the publication of *Bali Nyonga Today*, edited by Vincent Titanji (2016).

So, why is there a need to republish this volume? First, it aims to commemorate the fortieth anniversary of V.S. Galega II's passing into the ancestral realm. Second, it serves to honour the legendary scholars, both living and deceased, who dedicated considerable time and resources to publishing this volume in 1988. Ultimately, it aims to introduce the book to a broader audience by making it available in digital formats for future generations.

GALEGA II: FORTY YEARS DEPARTED

Born at the dawn of the 20th century in Bali, Galega II later became the first Western-educated king to ascend the throne in 1940, at a time of significant world events and profound societal change in his homeland and region. Originally published as a tribute to his leadership and legacy, this republication similarly honours that legacy, forty years after his passing. Remarkably, there is a surprising lack of scholarship on the legendary king, particularly given his notable contributions to Cameroon's political and socioeconomic spheres during the colonial and early postcolonial period. For example, his pioneering role as a traditional leader in the British Southern Cameroons could be the subject of potential extensive research—from his time in the Eastern Regional House of Assembly in Enugu, Nigeria, to the Southern Cameroons House of Chiefs and later as a prominent advocate for "reunification" and nation-building in the emerging Cameroon. By republishing this volume, we hope that younger and future generations of scholars, whether of Bali descent or beyond, will find inspiration in these pages to learn more about V.S. Galega II, his life, politics, and contributions to Bali society and Cameroon.

Similarly, forty years since his transition also marks forty years since his successor, Ganyonga III, ascended the throne. Republishing this book also serves as an account of what his successor inherited in terms of the vibrancy of Bali cultural institutions and traditions. As analysts would establish, both kings had and have had to contend with varying political eras and exigencies.

Figure 1. "The Fon of Bali, Galega II, seated in state in front of one of his important old ndop hangings which is held up by two Bali nobles. January 1981." Source: Venice and Alastair Lamb (1981). *Au Cameroun: Weaving-Tissage*

A TRIBUTE TO THE QUINTET

In May 2010, I had the distinct honour of delivering a keynote speech at the Bali Cultural Association USA, with Bali Nyonga's pioneering sociologist, Dr. Elias M. Nwana, in attendance. I reminded the audience of the significance of honouring our heroes while they are still among us and proceeded to highlight him for their recognition. Nwana, Ndangam, and Nti's (1978) documentation of Bali culture, published locally in 1978, merits special recognition for its significant contribution to safeguarding Bali cultural heritage. Before this landmark volume, available literature on Bali history and culture was mostly authored by British anthropologists and, previously, German ethnologists. In the metaphorical story of the hunt, Nwana and his colleagues became the "lions" that narrated the story of the hunt—as insiders, albeit in the language of the "hunters." As a trained sociologist and educationist, Dr. Nwana personally understood the importance of the written word in preserving and disseminating knowledge about Bali culture. While he never authored a monograph on a specific aspect of Bali culture, he wrote an autobiography and contributed a chapter to a volume I co-edited titled *Society and Change in Bali Nyonga* (Fokwang & Langmia, 2011). He also mentored numerous young Bali scholars who went on to research and write about aspects of Bali culture, even though many of these works remain unpublished. His seniority, erudition, and visionary role in contributing to the volume paying tribute to Galega II are deeply recognised and celebrated.

Gwannua Ndangam, a renowned linguist, educator, and knight of Bali (ŋkɔm), has played a crucial role in spreading knowledge about Bali cultural traditions. Having collaborated with Dr. Nwana on two previous works, including the volume paying tribute to V.S. Galega II, Ndangam later published a monograph, *Cultural Encounters* (2014), in which he skilfully explored topics such as the Bali worldview, kinship, political and cultural institutions, life cycle celebrations, and more. As one of the few surviving individuals knighted by Galega II, the republication of this volume celebrates his significant contributions not only to Bali scholarship but also to Bali society, both locally and in the diaspora. An account of the circumstances surrounding his receipt of Bali knighthood under Galega II would serve as a fitting tribute to the legendary king.

Vincent Titanji, a member of the royal family, celebrated scientist, and distinguished university administrator, played a pivotal role that culminated in the publication of *An Introduction to the Study of Bali-Nyonga*. His profound knowledge of Bali cultural institutions, as a member of some of the organs that govern Bali society, has allowed him to educate enthusiastic learners with his lucid and pointed descriptions of various aspects of Bali cultural heritage. Nearly three decades after the publication of *An Introduction,* he successfully coordinated and edited another landmark volume, *Bali Nyonga Today* (2016), which provided an opportunity for newer Bali scholars to explore some of the issues addressed in the 1988 volume. It is significant to note the exceptional quality of having someone who not only possesses firsthand knowledge of Bali culture but also writes about it with such eloquence. The republication of this volume is also a celebration of his enduring commitment to Bali scholarship and cultural preservation.

The republication of this anniversary volume probably would not have been possible without my interaction with Mathew B. Gwanfogbe, arguably Cameroon's most eminent historian of education. Discussions about republication took place as part of an effort to reissue two of his books that had originally been published in Cameroon. Their republication would enable them to reach a global audience in various formats. *An Introduction* became part of that discussion, thanks to Dr. Gwanfogbe, who arranged for a copy of the book to be sent to me. Although his scholarship primarily focused on broader issues beyond Bali culture, his publications intersected with aspects of Bali educational history (see Gwanfogbe, 2020). His introductory chapters on Bali migration history and geography are well-known and remain a reference point for many young historians and those interested in Bali Chamba history. This republication honours his memory and the lasting contributions he made in educating readers about Bali Nyonga history specifically.

This volume was especially fortunate to feature two distinguished linguists. Our second linguist, Adolf S. Lima, is renowned within the Bali community for his mentorship of younger linguists who later developed and adapted the old Mungaka alphabet to fit the modern Cameroon alphabet. A highly respected scholar and teacher, Lima had an illustrious career teaching linguistics at the universities of Yaoundé and Buea, where he supervised numerous students' work on Mungaka. This volume also honours his memory and his commitment to education.

OLD WINE IN NEW SKIN

Ultimately, the need to republish this volume is to, as the metaphor suggests, pour old, mature, and tasty wine into new skin – that is, to reinvent it for dissemination across new digital formats and thereby improve its accessibility for years to come. I became invested in this project not only because of its subject matter but especially because, as an anthropologist, I am convinced that the rich cultural knowledge we produce is only as valuable as it is accessible to those who need it. The aim here is to make this text widely accessible and affordable to all who wish to learn from its pages.

Readers of the original edition will find the anniversary version slightly edited for spelling, punctuation, and clarity. It was important during the process to preserve the original chapters as much as possible, and I am pleased to note that this has been achieved. Diagrams have been redrawn, and tables have been reformatted for improved flow. Photos have been embedded within the chapters where they best illustrate the issues discussed, rather than placed at the end of each chapter as in the original edition. Most importantly, the book includes a comprehensive index, which will help readers locate key ideas, names, and places. Finally, the book is available in paperback and digital formats (eBooks) on various platforms, including Google Books and Kindle. It will be widely accessible in academic libraries worldwide, especially in its digital format.

THE ESSAYS IN THIS VOLUME

This volume comprises six original essays of varying length and focus. Mathew B. Gwanfogbe begins with a *Geographical and Historical Introduction to Bali Nyonga.* He places Bali Nyonga within the southwestern limits of the Western Grasslands, providing extensive statistics and data for future geographers of Bali to build upon. His historical account of Chamba origins aligns with most scholarly literature, which situates their beginnings around the Cameroon-Nigeria border, on the plains of the Atlantika Mountains (also known as the Alantika Mountains). It examines plausible theories that may have prompted the outward migration of the Chamba Leko southwards and their eventual division into seven camps in the Bafu-Fondong region of the present-day Western Region of Cameroon, possibly in the late 1820s or early 1830s. From this fragmentation emerged Bali Nyonga, led by Princess Na'Nyonga, who later transferred leadership to her son, Nyongpasi. It was Nyongpasi, also called Fonyonga I, who established Bali Nyonga within its current territory in the 1830s. Gwanfogbe then details the reigns of successive Bali kings and devotes considerable attention to the rule of Galega II.

Gwanfogbe's historical outline provides rich material that intersects with interests in the history of the Western Grasslands and Cameroon history at large. For instance, a startling revelation is disclosed about King Bell of Douala's missive to Fonyonga II and Njoya of Bamum, inviting them to join him in initiating an anticolonial struggle against German colonial rule. Students of colonial Cameroon history, especially during the German period, would be particularly interested in examining the relationships between indigenous kings, their vassals, and German authorities.

Gwannua Ndangam's essay, *The Biography of V.S. Galega II (1906-1985),* is the most comprehensive account we have to date of Galega II's life. It details his paternal and maternal origins, early education within the Roman Catholic system, and eventual tutelage in secular education under the pioneering educator, Ba Gwankud-valla, whose daughter he would later marry. After completing his studies and entering the medical profession, Galega II ascended the throne in 1940 following a brief conflict with his half-brother, Tita Nyambi. Not much has been recorded about this royal dispute, which, for those familiar with Chamba history and African kingship generally, is not surprising. This brief exposé by Ndangam offers a fascinating foundation for interested historians to examine the circumstances of Galega II's rise and its implications.

The chapter then proceeds to catalogue Galega II's reign, focusing especially on his political life. Here, we see Galega II's initial involvement with the Kamerun National Congress (KNC) under Dr. E.M.L. Endeley, his fallout with the KNC after refusing to toe the party line on the question of Southern Cameroons' future, and his eventual siding with J.N. Foncha, whose political platform propelled the Southern Cameroons to "join" French Cameroon in 1961. The essay concludes with a brief narrative of his "private life," who, arguably, may have been the last Bali king to have over 200 children. It is an invaluable chapter that provides the outline for an extensive biography on Galega II.

Elias Nwana's chapter, *Economic and Social Setting of the Reign of Galega II (1940–1985),* offers a compelling analysis of the economic and social developments in Bali Nyonga, particularly in the post-World War II period. According to Nwana, following that devastating war, European recovery prompted numerous socio-economic changes in Bali Nyonga, including the establishment of the United Africa Company (UAC) in Mamfe, which subsequently expanded to include Bali as a branch. Advances in education, commerce, and infrastructure—especially the creation of an airstrip—helped connect Bali with the wider world and elevated its prominence as a leading kingdom in the Grasslands. The statement that Galega II "lived through change, solicited change, initiated, encouraged and promoted change" highlights a key theme of this chapter. Future economic and social historians of Bali are equipped with extensive knowledge to further their research.

In Chapter Four, V.P.K. Titanji critically examines *The Traditional Political Institution of Bali Nyonga.* For those interested in comparative traditional institutions within the Grasslands and specifically Bali Nyonga, this chapter offers profound insights into the different organs that wield political and religious power in Bali society. As readers will discover, a fine line separates the political and religious realms in the exercise of authority in most monarchical systems (see, for example, the divine rule of European kings prior to the Protestant Reformation). Titanji skilfully explores the origins of the Voma and Lela institutions, as well as their functions and operations. He also investigates the institution of palace retainers, known as *tsinted*, the office of knighthood called the *Kom*, other key regulatory bodies such as subchiefs (Fonte'), and the Ngumba. The latter part of his comprehensive essay details the normative procedures for installing a Bali king, focusing specifically on the coronation of Ganyonga III, successor to V.S. Galega II as Fon. Titanji's account arguably provides the most detailed insight into the exercise of political power in Bali, and his eyewitness testimony of Ganyonga III's installation remains a historic record to be valued for generations. Additionally, the inclusion of an extensive glossary is a notable bonus.

Many readers familiar with the Chamba kingdoms in the Cameroon Grasslands are often puzzled to learn that contemporary Bali Nyonga does not speak the same language as its kith and kin in the other kingdoms. This is where Adolf Sema Lima's chapter comes in.

His chapter, *The Mungaka Language: Its Development, Spread and Use,* critically examines the origins of Mungaka, reviewing three competing theories that aim to explain the language's origins. He concludes that the most convincing of these theories is the "historical and evolutionary theory" that explains its acquisition in the Bati/Bamum neighbourhood following the splintering of the Chamba groups in the Dschang area. Lima points out that there is "evidence that [Bati] is the mother-base of [Mungaka]. The Bati and Bamum languages share significant linguistic similarities, just as Mungaka and Bamum also share considerable affinity. Drawing on the historical and evolutionary theory, Lima concludes that "Mungaka was a sort of pidginized form of language derived from a fusion of the Bati and Bamum languages as well as some Bamileke languages such as Dschang and other related languages with which the Balis also had casual contact." His chapter further examines aspects of the structural linguistics of Mungaka, including its phonology – specifically, consonants, vowels, glottalized vowels, and tone. He then expends considerable effort in the remainder of his essay by exploring early efforts at the codification of Mungaka, secular publications and general literacy in Mungaka. He concludes his chapter by exploring naming conventions among the Bali with detailed examples of Mungaka and Mubako names.

Chapter Six, *The Origin of Mungaka: An Alternative View*, by Gwannua Ndangam, concludes the volume by examining other plausible theories about the origin of Mungaka. He narrows his theory to a gradual process of replacement, where Mubako was replaced by Mungaka-speaking children born from unions between Chamba men and Ba-Ti women. Na'Nyonga's contingent, he argues, was mainly composed of males who retreated after the "splinter" into the Ba-Ti neighbourhood, encountering a community of women whose male populations had been significantly decimated by the Bamum, creating a favourable opportunity for intermarriage. Predictably, the number of Mungaka-speakers grew while

Mubako-speakers gradually declined "through age and natural death or death at the war front."

Cumulatively, the essays in this volume provide readers with insights into Bali society in ways that no other volume had achieved at the time of its publication. It holds a unique place in history, having inspired numerous other monographs and essays that explore various aspects of Bali culture and society. More importantly, its contributions extend beyond Bali, shedding light on the evolution of politics and society in the Western Grasslands and Cameroon more broadly. We sincerely hope that these essays will motivate contemporary scholars and that the younger generation of Bali descendants will learn about the legendary king, Galega II, under whose leadership Bali society experienced significant change.

REFERENCES

Fokwang, J., & Langmia, K. (Eds.). (2011). *Society and Change in Bali Nyonga: Critical Perspectives*. Langaa Research and Publishing.

Gwanfogbe, M. B. (2020). *Basel Mission Education in Cameroon: 1886-1968*. Spears Media Press.

Ndangam, G. (2014). *Cultural Encounters: Society, Culture and Language in Bali Nyonga From the 19th Century*. Instantpublisher.com.

Nwana, E. M., Ndangam, A. F., & Nti, D. F. (Eds.). (1978). *The Living Culture of Bali-Nyonga. The Lela Festival. The First Attempt of a Series of Documentation on the Bali-Nyonga Tradition.*

Titanji, V., Gwanfogbe, M., Nwana, E., Ndangam, G., & Lima, A. S. (1988). *Introduction to the study of Bali-Nyonga: A Tribute to his Royal Highness Galega II, Traditional Ruler of Bali-Nyonga From 1940-1985*. Stardust Printers.

Titanji, V. P. K. (Ed.). (2016). *Bali Nyonga Today: Roots, Cultural Practices and Future Perspectives*. Spears Media Press.

HRH Galega II, Fon of Bali Nyonga, 1940–1985.
Credit: Hans Knöpfli

1

Geographical and Historical Introduction of Bali Nyonga

M.B. Gwanfogbe

Bali Nyonga is one of the five Chamba Kingdoms of the North West Province of Cameroon. It is one of the subdivisions of Mezam. Bali Nyonga is located within 9°40'E and 10°50'E longitude. It extends from latitude 5°50'N to 6°10'N of the equator. The subdivision is bounded in the North and East by Bamenda Central subdivision, in the South by Batibo subdivision and in the West by Mbengwi subdivision.

The Bamenda-Mamfe road passes through Bali. From this principal road, there are many secondary roads leading to villages within the subdivision and beyond. There is also an airport that connects Bali to other towns.

The Bali Nyonga subdivision covers an area of about 191 sq. km (Conrade, 1974), with a population density then of 125 persons per square kilometre. Presidential Decree No. 66/DF/433 of August 26,1966, initially made Bali an administrative district within the Mezam Division. But owing to several intervening, dynamic factors, the government decided by Decree No. 79/469 of 14th November 1979 to raise it to the status of subdivision.

Many geographical factors have enabled the Bali subdivision to develop relatively faster than other chiefdoms in the Western

Grassfields. These include the relief structure, drainage pattern, climate, vegetation, and soil.

The Bali Nyonga subdivision lies at the foot of the Bambutu plateau, which is the southwest limit of the western highlands. To a large extent, the subdivision is separated from its north-eastern neighbours by an escarpment, while her north-eastern neighbours: Nsongwa, Mbatu, Chomba, Mbu and Pinyin are located on the limits of the Bambutu plateau. Thus, Bali is a low-lying region or a basin receiving the rivers from the rest of the highland places. These rivers bring alluvium that add to the fertility of the subdivision making it the grain winner of the province.

It is important to note that in spite of its basin structure, Bali has also highlands with peaks such as Olulu (1,467m), Mbutu, Kobpin (1,388m) Mbeluh, Kubat, Fukang (1,535m), in the northeast and southeast regions. The land slopes gently from these regions into the West region and has some highlands such as Ntanko'o (1,348m), Gawola and Gwenjang.

There are also broad river valleys generally oriented Northeast/Southwest, following the topographical structure. Some of these include Naka, Tob, Mbufung, Mantum, Boh-Montoh, Sepua and Kontan.

As earlier stated, Bali is drained by many rivers rising from the highlands of the Northeast and East of the region. Most of the rivers are intermittent, whereas some are the main tributaries of big rivers. An example is the River Naka, which is an important tributary of the River Menchum.

Although Bali belongs to the humid tropical zone, the rainfall is moderated by the altitude and distance from the sea. Rainfall varies between 2,000 and 3,000 mm per annum. The rains are brought by the southwest monsoon trade winds, which flow unperturbed over the Bali land but sometimes cannot climb the escarpment owing to the high altitude, thereby enabling Bali to receive relief rains because of its structure. The rainfall is seasonal, between March and October. The dry season starts from November and ends in mid-March, recording little rain.

Owing to the basin structure and the varying seasons, temperatures are unsteady. A maximum of 31°C and a minimum of 12°C have been registered (Titanji W. B., 1984). These varying climatic conditions, favour the cultivation of crops in both the warm and cold areas. An example is the cultivation of Robusta coffee in the warm areas and Arabica coffee in the cold (escarpment) areas of the subdivision. It also favours both the cultivation of tubers and cereals.

The traditional vegetation cover is savannah with gallery forests and tall grass along the valleys. But human activities have interfered a lot with the vegetation. It is now possible to find large expanses of eucalyptus forests on the hills and large raffia palm forests in the depressions. There is also a forest reserve at Mantum, which, along with the eucalyptus forest, supplies the people with a lot of wood for building and furniture as well as fuel.

Bali is at the foot of extinct volcanic mountains. Consequently, it belongs to the volcanic soils. These rich soils, as well as the alluvium brought by the rivers and the rather long rainy season, have altogether favoured two farming seasons in Bali. Meanwhile, the hill slopes which are generally underlined by lateritic soils are less fertile but enable the growth of grass on which cattle graze.

It will therefore be noticed from the foregoing brief geographical introduction that Bali subdivision lies on a favourable relief feature and it is blessed with a good drainage pattern that does not only supply water to the people but also brings alluvium to add to its fertility. The climate and vegetation are a combination of enviable human and animal attractions, and the geological underpinnings add to the basic soil requirements for agriculture. It must have therefore been a serious attraction for man's habitation since time immemorial. Such an attraction must have led to many groups scrambling for its occupation so much so that it is difficult today to state who were the original occupants. Our attempt to trace the outline history of Bali, however, will lead us to identify some of the recent occupants of this admirable region.

HISTORY

It should be noted right from the start that besides its geographical attraction, it is seemingly clear that Bali has equally attracted many historians and other social scientists researching on the Western Grassfields. Compared to her neighbours and her Chamba kith and kins, much has been written about the history of Bali Nyonga. But it is apparently clear that in spite of their good intentions, many of the writers portray inadequate cultural knowledge of the people. Consequently, their interpretations of the history generally leave much to be desired since such interpretations have to depend largely on a good knowledge of the peoples' belief systems and aspirations. It is hoped, however, that the involvement of Bali indigenes in research on their culture and history will reveal new elements and throw more light on the attractive history of the people. It will enlighten the public on who they are, where they come from, how they arrived at their present settlement, and their life since settling there. What we are presenting here are but the highlights of their history without any elaborate developments.

Origin

It has generally been accepted by scholars (Kaberry, 1961; Chilver, 1961; Soh, 1978; Hunt, 1925; Jeffreys, 1962, etc.) that Bali Nyonga belongs to the Chamba Leko group that migrated from Chamba around River Faro on the Cameroon-Nigeria borders. Soh and Mohammadou (1978) hold that the Chamba people settled in the Benue plain around circa 1600, but where they came from at the time is not yet clearly known. Some traditions hold that they came from Japan and that Chamba is the deformed pronunciation of Japan. Others hold that they came from Indonesia because of the

Bali in Indonesia. Both hypotheses are certainly untrue because of the marked racial and cultural differences that exist between the Chamba and the Far Eastern people. A more commonly held opinion is the fact that the Chamba came from Arabia. This may also be dismissed because it is akin to the Hamitic hypothesis. It is, however, seemingly true that they were one of the Sudanese groups settled around Lake Chad before or around the 10th century A.D., which must have decided to move south as a result of further desertification and increased famine. It could have equally been one of those groups that decided to keep off from the ambitious expanding Kanuri empire. If this hypothesis is true, then the Chamba Southwards movement must have been much earlier than the beginning of the 17th century (Soh, 1978). But if they migrated to the area as a result of the exploitation of the subsequent bustling of the Borno empire, then it is probable to agree with their settlement to date from the beginning of the 17th century which is concurrent with the reign of Umar the Warrior and Ali his son c. 1623–1680 of the Borno empire.

However, the Bata migration from Southern Borno must have equally resulted from a further Borno expansion. This group demonstrated a more centralised system of government but co-existed for quite a long time with the Chambas and their neighbours such as the Vere, Koutin or Pere, Dourou, Dwayo, etc. It is possible to believe that both the Chambas and Bata must have been part of the Kanem-Borno empire and both resisted the growing influence of Islamic rule in the empire. It should be noted that since the 14th century the Kanuri empire was largely influenced by Islam and non-Muslims stood to pay severe taxes. This must have caused most of the Sudanese non-Muslim groups to migrate. While the Chamba and others migrated earlier, the Bata came later and in a larger number following the commercially motivated and expansionist Islamic wars under Idris B. Alooma (1571–1603) of the Borno empire.

Nevertheless, the arrival of the Bata people had further incidence on the history of the region. In view of their number and freshness from war, they were prepared to conquer and subdue their predecessors on the land. Their target was the fertile areas of the plain on both banks of River Faro and south of River Dewo. In addition, it is believed that famine as a result of no rain for four consecutive years (Soh, 1978) led to Chamba-Leko departure westward across the Atlantika mountains under the leadership of Loya Garbosa into the Junkun country, still in the Benue. Here they subdued the declining kingdom of Kororofa in the first half of the 18th century. It should be noted that Kororofa once conquered all the Hausa states. Meanwhile, the Chamba Daka did not accompany them.

From the Junkun region, they sojourned southwards into Kontcha, where they concluded an alliance with the Buti (Soh 1978). They continued eastwards into the Ngaoundere region and absorbed the Kufad, which was a clan of the Mbum who still form a large population of the Adamawa province today. The Fulani jihad must have finally affected their final departure from this area since Soh holds that they left Ngaoundere about 1815. They moved south-westwards through Banyo where they incorporated large numbers of Tikars commonly known in Bali as Tikali.

It should be noted that Chamba-Fulani relations had lasted for long. Fulani infiltration in the Fombina region must have been around the 16th century when the Borno empire was at its climax, although Muslim infiltration was before the 10th century A.D. through the Trans-Sahara trade routes. As cattle rearers, they must have extended to the savannah landscape of Fombina where the Chamba had settled for long. Oral traditions equally give the Chamba a Fulani origin. This is linked with the Hamitic theory, which is associated with great kingdoms, empires and the civilisation of Arabia. On the contrary, it is more possible to believe that when the Fulani settled, they must have had a long peaceful coexistence with the Chamba during which cultural and social relations yielded many similarities. Marriages and other socialising factors must have brought the two ethnic groups close. It is possible that the dressing and musical similarities (Danga and Lela fluting and drumming as well as horse-riding and flag-bearing) are products of this socialisation.

However, whereas the Fulani remains a distinctly cattle breeder, the Chamba, through his belief system and reaction to the world around him, proves to have been a farmer and hunter for long. It is believed that "the Chamba initiated the Fulani into the art of manipulating certain arms especially the bow and arrow" (Soh, 1978) as well as horse riding, a practice which has lasted for long in the area.

This good relation was obviously destroyed by the Fulani ambition to establish a Holy Empire under the pretext of Islamic purification led by Usman dan Fodio, with Adama as his local lieutenant. Chamba was attacked by Fulani from many directions. Some Chamba clans submitted, while others resisted and fled. Those who travelled south-eastwards were the founders of the north-west Chamba chiefdoms. They were led by Gawolbe (circa 1790–1836) (Chilver and Kaberry, 1970) and besides the real Chamba elements there were large contingents of Koutin or Peli (Pere), Mbum, Buti and Tikars that followed. Chilver holds that future King Galega I of Bali Nyonga was born in Banyo shortly before the departure of Gawolbe from Chamba for a further southward migration. This movement is believed to have occurred around 1825.

Gawolbe led the Bare (as the Bamum and other Tikars still call Bali) South-eastwards, waging wars against many groups. Mohammadou Eldridge states that the Bare cavalry launched an attack on Bamum as they descended into their region. However, oral traditions hold that the Chamba settled for a while before attacking the Bamum. Tradition suggests that the Chamba sought to exploit an existing friction between the Bamum and their Bati

(Ti or Pati) neighbours to launch an attack on Bamum. However, they were not successful in subjugating the Bamum but amalgamated some of the Bati referred to by Chilver and Kaberry (1965) as "Ti Gawolbe" and moved further south to Bagam, which they conquered. Thereafter, they moved to Bamenjinda and Babaju (Bawaju) and then into Bamenda, fighting on their way with the Bafreng, Mankon, Bafut, Meta, Moghamo, Bapinyin and eastwards to Dschang. Many traditions in these areas still remember vividly the Gawolbe led cavalry and bowmen who were the first to introduce horses in the Grassfields; hence horses are generally known as *Nyambani*, *Nyambane* (i.e., Bali beast).

It is noteworthy to point out here that the Chamba itinerary is not unanimously agreed upon. It is also held that there was another entry further north because they are said to have sacked the former Banso headquarters of Kovifem. This version does not seem to be true because no Bali tradition makes mention of it. Kovifem might also be a mistake for Kufom which will be explained later.

However, the southward movement of the Chamba was limited by the increasing forest vegetation which their horses could not resist. Thus, after camping for a while, they moved eastwards without passing through the present site of Bali Nyonga. In Dschang, they found an admirable landscape suitable for settlement. But the natives of the land put up a severe resistance which ended up with the death of Gawolbe at the battle of Bafu-Fundong (also Bafu-Fondong) near Djuitisa. Djuitisa presently has a large CDC tea estate on part of the coveted land. The Chamba then moved north-westwards and camped around Bagam in order to reorganise and select a new leader.

The Split

It is very probable that the heir apparent, Gangsin, was weak and unpopular. He was the only son born when Gawolbe became king. If he were powerful and competent enough, he would have been able to weld together the Chamba people and establish a strong and united kingdom.

Kingship in the Bali tradition is a prestigious and highly coveted position. It usually attracts the attention of many candidates. Thus, the succession of Gawolbe was not going to be easily settled because of the many postulants to the throne. The tension produced by the rivalry for the throne led to the split of Bali-Chamba into seven principalities.

1. **Bali-Gangsin**, known as Donep, settled southeast of Bali Kumbat.
2. **Bali-Gaso (Gashu)**, otherwise known as Gasonep, was led by Ga-Nyam. They settled for a while near the present site of Bali-Gham before sojourning northward to settle East of Bali-Kumbat.
3. **Bali-Gham**, known as Nepgavilbi, was led by Ga-Sanga. They moved to Bagham-Nindeng where they acquired the locational -name of Bali-Gham. They later on moved to their present site.
4. **Bali-Kumbat** otherwise known as Nepkolbi, was led by Galega (an influential retainer who knew too many palace secrets). This was the largest group and wielded great powers among the Chamba. They moved North-westward, waging wars against Bambili, Bambui and the Tikars of the Ndop plain. Finally, they defeated the Bamukumbit and settled on their hilltop position.
5. **Bali-Muti**: Kaberry and Chilver state that they travelled north via Wum and settled in Takum, which is currently located in the Gongola State of Nigeria.
6. **Bali-Konntan**: They travelled south-westward and settled at Kufom, in the present Bali Nyonga subdivision. They were later assimilated by Bali Nyonga. This partially explains why Bali Nyonga, unlike all other Bali states has

two flags (Tutuwan).

7. **Bali Nyonga**, was led by Nyongpasi, the son of Princess Na'nyonga, wife of Samjewa. Na'nyonga must have been queen or regent before handing over to her son. This is supported by the suppression of Voma, a male cult always headed by the Fon, which was reinstated in Bali Nyonga only during the reign of Galega I. Her son became Fonyonga I. He led his group first to the environs of Bamum and must have renewed relations with the Bati who were obviously enemies to or recalcitrant subjects of the Bamum. It is not yet clear as to why they again left the place, but it is possible to suggest that an attempted allied war with the Bati against the Bamum must have failed to avail them of any dividends. It is also clear that on leaving the Bamum country for the Bamenda area, they must have taken along with them some of the Bati people. This is possibly the beginning of the Bali Nyonga and Bati coexistence and the initial beginning of the Mungaka language in Bali Nyonga.

However, as we shall see in detail below, the Bali Nyonga people moved southwestward and settled at Kufom three kilometres northeast of the Cameroon Protestant College, Bali (former /settlement). From there, they raided the Widikum principalities, which occupied their present site and settled there. It was also at this time that they absorbed the Bali-Konntan and many other Widikum groups.

The Bali-Chamba split is significant in the history of the Western Grassfields of the 19th century. This is evident in the inter-relations of the various Bali states as well as their relationship with their neighbours. Within the various groups, there was endless rivalry. Tradition holds that Bali-Kumbat waged several wars on the other states with the aim of subjecting them. Thus, the split caused endless fighting, which must have contributed to their continuous movements before the final settlement.

However, the split reduced the impact of the frequency of their raids on the people of the Western Grassfields. It is believed that if these people remained united, they could have terrorised and even displaced many people in the Western grassland. Despite the split, the different states still caused significant damage to the people they encountered and renewed migrations among those who had already settled.

Another pertinent point to note is the fact that the split could have been avoided if the powerful Gawolbe had succeeded in settling in Djuitisa. But why could they not settle before then? Tradition holds it that the extensive travelling was because they were in search of a land similar to the one they left in Chamba, i.e., land along a river. It is also believed that they needed an area large enough to accommodate their numbers, free from pestilence, and fertile enough to avoid the occurrence of famine. This opinion seems to gain more credibility.

Notwithstanding the split, traditions in most places of the Grassfields still popularly point at the Bali Chamba as warriors. After their split, the small states continued to prove tough and prone to warmongering. We earlier mentioned some of the wars they waged to conquer the places they finally settled. Yet after settling, their histories abound with several wars of further conquests, domination, subjugation of the conquered people and consolidation of their conquests. The history of Bali Nyonga from its creation will serve as an example of the Chamba lifestyle after Gawolbe,

BALI NYONGA UNDER FONYONGA I, C. 1835–1856

As earlier mentioned, Nyongpasi, the son of Princess Na'nyonga, first child of Gawolbe on arrival to power, became King Fonyonga I of Bali Nyonga following the schism which occurred after the death of Gawolbe. He led his people to Tsen, also known as Kuti or Kupare as the Bamum refer to the area which is located in the Southern part of the Bamum region. It should be remembered here that his grandfather, Gawolbe, had already established good relations with them. Here, they entered into an alliance with the Bati who were traditional enemies of the Bamum. This enmity is still popular in Bali Nyonga traditions today, for there is a popular ballad which runs thus:

Nkang mbab, Nkang musing
Nchotu mfa mfa'mon
Mfa'mon que yi nkwet-nkwet
Nga nque yia ma' ku lanwoe
Mbi to mbitso' mbu' lung
Kulung-kulung-kulung eh!
Bati ka wat Bamum eh!
Bamum ka wat Bati eh!

Meaning:

I fried mice and birds for lunch
Gave their heads to the maid
Who took her share and ate
But I took mine and set a trap with it on a rock
When I returned,
Lo! there was a chimpanzee on the trap
Singing and playing a fiddle:
The Bati went to war with the Bamum
The Bamum went to war with the Bati.

This song illustrates the tense atmosphere that prevailed between Bamum and Bati upon the arrival of the Bali Nyonga. From Tsen, and with the Bati allies, Fonyonga I waged a series of wars against the eastern Bamileke states such as Bangante, Bansoa, Bamunju, etc. He also fought against the kingdom of Fumban but failed to conquer King Mbwombwo, whose army had gained great fighting skill during the Bamum/Banyo war of 1840. Bamum went on the offensive and attacked the Ba'ni unexpectedly. This unannounced attack led to Bali Nyonga's further departure from Kuti in c. 1848 along with their BaNten allies and Bamileke subjects. They stopped for a while in Bagam plain, where Fonyonga re-organised his army before moving to the Bamenda area. It is held by P.M. Kaberry and E.M. Chilver that hopes to settle in Bamum could not be realised because Fonyonga disagreed with Bali Kumbat, which was a larger and more powerful group. At Bamenda, they made a blood treaty with the Fon of Bafreng and stayed on for seven years before pursuing their Konntan brethren at Kufom. There, too, they defeated Bali Konntan and amalgamated it with their Mbatu, also known as Mudum and Kenyang subjects (Ba Ntanka), in 1855 and settled. In 1856, Fonyonga I died (Soh, 1978).

Fonyonga I's reign proved to be the shortest of the first four monarchs of the Bali Nyonga kingdom as we shall notice. However, it was one of uncertainty, characterised by wars and frequent movements as well as multi-tribal subjects with a heterogeneous linguistic problem. Fonyonga's ability to wield together this group and single-handedly threaten great kingdoms such as Mbwombwo's Bamum, which had resisted Banyo jihad attacks, proves that he was a competent leader. It should be remembered that his legitimacy to the throne from the beginning presented problems. Yet he consolidated his powers and was able to establish a firm authority over his people. He is therefore largely responsible for the establishment of the Bali Nyonga state, which eventually became the centre of political activities in the Grassfields at the advent of Europeans. He paved the way for succeeding rulers to give Bali Nyonga the prominence it had in the Grassfields before and during the colonial era. He is, therefore, a founder who will never be ignored by all descendants of the Bali Nyonga chiefdom.

BALI NYONGA UNDER GALEGA I C. 1856–1901

If Fonyonga I was the founder of Bali Nyonga, then Galega I was the organiser and consolidator of the kingdom. He introduced vital military and internal reforms that projected Bali Nyonga as a great state at the advent of the Europeans. His competence to settle a people who had been sojourning for almost four decades and his ability not only to stop continuous attacks from hostile enemies but also to conquer more people and to enlarge the kingdom leaves one to conclude that he was one of extra-ingenuity. It is pertinent to note that, like his contemporaries in Europe, he fought for unity, and his efforts ultimately achieved absolute success.

In the region, there were two organised and powerful states: Bafut and Mankon which were both threatening to Bali. However, Bali was feared as mounted warriors whose recent raiding and pillaging wars scared any adventurer from attacking them. In addition, military pacts with Bafreng and Bamendankwe were comforting. Another threat they had to encounter was from their kinsmen—Bali Kumbat. Bali Nyonga's defeat of the Bali Kumbat will be elaborated later. Suffice it now to note the fact that their defeat gave Bali Nyonga greater assurance and projected Galega I as yet the greatest monarch among the Chamba states in the region.

From Kufom, Galega waged wars against the Widikum states in their present site. Some were allowed to stay provided they agreed to supply labour and regular tribute. Others fled to take refuge in neighbouring states. According to oral tradition (Bali Historical Society, 1961), Fonyonga II, the future king, was born in Kufom. Galega transferred his people to the present site when the future ruler was 18 years old. It is therefore possible to date Bali Nyonga's transfer to its present site, effective from circa 1873.

The Fon lived at the heart of the state, known as Nted, whose immediate precincts were occupied by his retainers or *Nchinteds*. Thereafter were clusters of compounds built in quarters headed by contingent leaders: Fonte of Won, Ngiam, Tikali, Buti, Kundem,

Kefad, Ti, Munyam, Foleng, Set, etc. Galega undertook serious political reorganisation and gave a sense of direction to all his subjects.

He did not, however, neglect his predecessors' usual practice of raiding for expansion. Some of the victims were kept as labour for developing Bali, while others were sold for guns and gunpowder in the markets in Sabe (Mamfe) and Bamenjinda. They captured slaves from the north and sold them to the south to neighbours of the River Manyu (Cross River). These were the Ejagham and Banyang trade allies. It is important to note here that there was huge traffic in guns, gunpowder, salt and cloth in exchange for slaves, ivory and meat on the Manyu River.

At the time of the arrival of Europeans in 1889, Bali Nyonga, under Galega I, was ruled from the forest borders, with boundaries that extended south to the present-day Manyu people and northeast into the Bamileke chiefdoms. All rivals and enemies had been exterminated.

GALEGA I AND BALI KUMBAT

Shortly after settling on the present site, they severely defeated the Bali Kumbat, who had persistently attacked Bali Nyonga. At the battles of Paila and Ngwa'ndikang in c. 1875, most of the war leaders of Bali Kumbat are said to have been killed. Oral sources further have it that the fleeing Fon of Bali-Kumbat was caught by Bafreng allies and brought to Bali Nyonga. The Bali Kumbat/Bali Nyonga confrontations are particularly significant because of the subsequent differences that emanated between Bali Nyonga and the rest of the Chamba kinsmen, giving Bali Nyonga pre-eminence over all others. First of all, a linguistic difference secured as a result of the necessity to distinguish the troops and communicate with them without letting out their secrets to their enemies. It is true that Bali Nyonga's sojourning in Kuti (Tsen) and their amalgamation of a large number of Bati followers helped to introduce Mungaka to Bali Nyonga. But it is certain that a more systematic teaching of the language was organised as part of the military preparation to thwart the Bali Kumbat aggressions.[1]

The confrontations are also significant because they were determining factors for Bali Nyonga assimilation policy. Realising that they were numerically inferior to the Bali Kumbat, the Bali Nyonga rulers adopted a policy of assimilating their enemies and those who offered to join them in order to counter the strength of their enemies and to fight back whenever necessary. Mubako was equally strange and dissimilar to the population of the Grassfields which was dominated by the Tikars. The policy of adopting Mungaka, which was widely spoken in the entire Western Grassfields, was also commercially very profitable to the Bali Nyonga people. It is not, therefore, surprising that Bali Nyonga has emerged as the strongest and largest of the Chamba states in the 20th century.

One important political and military innovation during Galega's reign was the establishment of some princes as war leaders. A number of Galega's sons competed for battle honours and leadership. Two of the important ones were Yabala Njingwadnyam popularly known as Tita Nji born at Bafreng during the migration in the 1840s and Voma Gwenjang Mbo also known as Tita Gwenjang or Tita Mbo, born in Kufom c. 1855. The latter became king after Galega I.

GALEGA I AND REFORMS

Having defeated both internal and external enemies, Galega and his subjects settled down to domestic reforms. These included the establishment and consolidation of political institutions, as well as the creation of a government powerful enough to manage the growing empire. This was so skilfully done that the old-time warriors were gradually transformed into great administrators.

1 See Chapter five for further explanation.

The Fon became the central authority overseeing the functioning of government in all areas, under various members of the government, and coordinating both domestic and foreign policies of the kingdom. This organisation led Bali Nyonga to become more powerful and influential in establishing its authority over the conquered surrounding states, which were obliged to have their peace only on condition that they regularly paid tribute to Bali Nyonga. Consequently, before the arrival of the Germans, Bali Nyonga was enjoying a splendid and unchallenged authority in the region. Thus, the conception that Bali Nyonga's powerful role in the Grassfields was a product of the German colonial administration is false.

GALEGA I AND COLONIAL GERMANY

While Bali Nyonga was consolidating her influence in the grasslands, the Germans were doing the same in the coastal region and seeking an entry point into the interior. Five years after planting the German colonial flag on the coast (1884), the Germans found themselves in Bali Nyonga (1889).

Galega I and the First European Visitor

Dr. Eugen Zintgraff made the first European appearance in the Grassfields. Zintgraff was a German, born in Düsseldorf in 1858. He had joined the European bandwagon of imperialist exploration, usually termed from the Euro-centric perception as voyages of discovery or civilising exploration, at the age of 26. He participated in the exploration of Lower Congo in a team led by Chavenne in 1884. Thereafter, he failed to gain government support to explore Kamerun from the Ubangi. In 1885, he made some probing explorations around the River Wouri. In company of Zeuner he started the German station at Barombi near Kumba in the Southwest Province of Cameroon in January 1888. Rudin points out that during this period, he was determined to establish a trade route linking Calabar and the Benue lands, which Beecroft and other imperialists had failed to accomplish in 1842. It must be remembered here that the commercial interest of Germany was at the forefront of their explorations. Zintgraff and his countrymen saw the route as a means by which the great palm oil trade of West Africa could be harnessed and, more particularly, as a source of labour for the coastal plantations. These motives led to government support for Zintgraff.

It was during the governorship of Von Soden, the first governor of German Kamerun (1885-1891) that Zintgraff had his approval and support and left Douala via the Mungo River by canoe to Barombi from where he continued on foot through Nguti, Bayang, Difang, Fotabe, Tinto, Babessong to Bali. He took off from Douala with 175 carriers comprised of 100 Lagosians and 75 Monrovians (Hunt, 1925). He, however, had a Grassfields interpreter called Muyenga who had earlier served Flegel during his exploration of the Adamawa region and thereafter became a servant of Prince Manga Bell. On the way, there was resistance from various Cameroon groups, which, however, were in many cases defeated because of the unpreparedness of the people and the heavy and sophisticated firearms of the intruders. This led to an increase in the number of carriers as they advanced inland.

On January 16th, 1889, Zintgraff and his gang arrived in Bali. They were welcomed at the frontier by Galega's army led by important dignitaries. Zintgraff remarked that these were the first Africans to look at him straight in the eye. On arrival at the palace, Zintgraff was conducted to the piazza, which was in his words, "a gently rising square hidden by finely woven mat walls awl over-hung by shady trees" (Chilver 1966). Kibot states that Zintgraff had to wait for some time before "the paramount king, Galega I" could appear. His appearance was a majestic and highly impressive occasion that pulled heavy applauses not only from the citizens but equally from Zintgraff and his followers, who were greatly amazed by the dignity and splendour in which the "Black leader" lived. He was dressed in an ostentatious dark-red burnous with large, ample folds that gave him a befitting elegance and conjured admiration and respect.

Zintgraff's stop in Bali, unlike in all other stages of the expedition, seemed to have been more significant. It is worth noting that although this was the first European physical encounter with Bali, echoes of their conquest and commercial prowess were already known along the coast. The popularity and the paramountcy of Galega I had been carried far and wide by traders and slaves. Thus, Zintgraff was expecting to meet a commanding people with whom German ambition in the conquest of the Grassfields could be accomplished. But Zintgraff was not certain, however, of the Bali reaction to a friendly initiative. It is also clear to note that Zintgraff must have sent emissaries to Bali to announce his arrival to Galega I. This is true because Galega I had to send a large entourage to conduct him to his palace.

Kibot states that Zintgraff was very impressed with Galega I, and he became "convinced he had found a man of rare rational character who would not only be loyal but also an interesting ally in all matters of interest." But as Soh discerns, Galega was "very shrewd and Galega's total competence in foreign policy manoeuvring to obtain their military might to the advantage of Bali Nyonga and thus consolidating Bali imperial gains." This shrewdness and Galega's total competence in foreign policy operations resulted in the establishment of a double treaty proposed by both parties. The blood oath alliance, a traditional African symbol of a treaty, was advocated for by Galega I before Zintgraff continued his pursuit in Adamawa. Galega swore and said:

> You came here like a little chicken into my house, whiteman, and I would have easily killed you and taken your valuables. But since you have been staying with me, I have seen and learnt something of the fashion of the whites. Yet there are many people around me

> advising me to kill you. But do not fear, for I will not harm you nor allow others to harm you, for it is better to obtain the knowledge of the whites and have them as friends to our lasting benefit, than to make a short-lived advantage of them by robbery (Chilver, 1967).

Zintgraff on his part equally admired not just the people and their ruler and the clean atmosphere but also the good climate, the fertile land and its nearness to the sources of ivory (Kibot, 1980). He therefore decided to establish a German station in Bali, which at that time was considered by Bali as a German embassy and not a colonial administrative headquarters. This was called "Baliburg" and became the first German (European) colonial station in the entire Grassfields.

The building of the station was designed and constructed by Bali architects, as the materials employed were all made of local materials, which European builders could not manipulate. It was at the end of the building that Zintgraff continued on his mission to Adamawa on 25th April 1889, after more than three months' stay in Bali.

Zintgraff travelled through Bande (Mankon), Bafut, Bebabefang, Takum, Ibi, and arrived Wukari in May 1889. Then, through Jebbu, Bakundi to Gashaka, and then to Yola, and back through Gashaka, Taku, Bum, Bikom, Bamungo (also known as Babungo in Ndop), Bambui, Bamenda-Nkwe to Bali in November 1889. This itinerary is intended to illustrate the brevity of Zintgraff's stays in these places compared to his extended stay with Galega. It is aimed at demonstrating his attachment to the Bali allies, whom he intended to exploit for German benefit, and his detachment from the eventual German foes who would resist colonialism. However, upon his return, he stayed for another six weeks before departing for Douala and subsequently travelling to Germany. The six weeks were a period of feasting, renewal of faith in the two parties and time long enough for Zintgraff to recuperate from the long journey. Zintgraff left Bali on December 24th 1889, for Germany via Douala and Sao Tome. He made a strong report on the newly acquired empire and encouraged Germany to take advantage of his discoveries. The German foreign office thus sponsored a second trip in 1890.

GALEGA I AND THE SECOND VISIT OF EUROPEANS

Zintgraff came back to Bali on 9 December 1890 in the company of Nehber, a representative of Thormahlen Company, Caulwell, who led the caravan, Carstensen an old soldier and an experienced explorer, Tiedt an experienced sailor as well as 375 carriers. It was a joy for both Galega and Zintgraff to meet again. The Germans stayed this time for seven months, during which they signed a treaty of protection with Galega, which had the following provisions:

1. To transfer to Zintgraff as commissioner representing the Imperial Government all power of life and death, war and peace in Galega's lands.
2. The obligation of Galega to give effect by all means in his power to German orders to hold his forces in readiness for war and to fight only on German instructions and with German permission.
3. The establishment, recognition and protection of Galega's position as paramount chief of surrounding tribes of the northern Cameroons hinterland.
4. The division of taxes to be raised from neighbouring tribes and fixed duty payable by caravans passing through Bali districts from the hinterland between the German Government for direct government costs and Galega as official payment.
5. The reservation of all customs and taxation decision to Zintgraff as commissioner (E.M. Chilver in Prosser Gifford

1967).

The treaty was typical of all other colonial treaties signed during the period when African rulers are said to have surrendered their independence to European intruders. The reasons for this behaviour on the part of African rulers have been a long-standing topic of debate among historians. Some people present the threat of the Europeans. Others state that it was achieved through the lure of European goods. While others hold that African leaders were less intelligent and uncivilised. It is, however, a combination of these and many other factors. But the particular case of Galega I seemed to have been situated in his strong faith in the sincerity of the white man with whom he had taken a blood vow not to harm or deceive each other. He considered all subsequent transactions with the white man to be based on absolute sincerity and for the benefit of both parties. This is an indication of the good moral standards by which the people lived before the European intoxication of the society. Regardless of the reasons, Zintgraff's intentions were not understood by Galega. Galega least believed he was surrendering his powers to the Germans. He never dreamt that his white friend would eventually want to rule him rather than collaborate with him. He understood that the treaty sought the consolidation of his Grassfields empire under his absolute sovereignty,

A significant element in the treaty negotiation is the language that was employed; The five-clause treaty is said to have undergone a number of interpretations from Pidgin English to Vai (language spoken by Monrovian carriers) and from Vai to Bali and vice versa. It should be noted that Pidgin English was the commercial language on the West Coast of Africa in the 19th century. It is certain that all Germans adventuring on the West Coast had to learn Pidgin English. Although the Vai boys could speak Pidgin English, it is clear that they could not, in a few weeks, speak any of the local Bali languages at the time. They must have been some fake interpretations involved. The role of interpreters in giving wrong information during the colonial period has been confirmed by many scholars. Some interpreters did not understand one of the languages in which they were working. Some only partially understood the European language or Pidgin English but pretended to be very knowledgeable in the languages. It must have been this kind of interpretation that took place.

Notwithstanding any interpretation we may give the treaty, it remains clear that the Bali reactions to it in subsequent years demonstrate their earlier understanding of its implications.

GALEGA I AND GERMAN AGGRESSION IN THE GRASSFIELDS

Shortly after the Bali-German treaty, the Germans started their pacification wars in the Grassfields. It all started when the kingdoms of Bafut and Mankon disrespected German demands for trade and killed two of the Vai boys on Christmas Day of 1890 (Dibaw, p. 31). This led to war in which Bali and Zintgraff allied against Mankon and Bafut on 28 January 1891. In spite of the huge damage suffered by Mankon and Bafut, Zintgraff suffered the loss of his four companions.

Following this war, Zintgraff arranged for Germany to equip the Bali army with 2000 rifles, which arrived Bali on 23 August 1891. Although these guns were not eventually used for the intended purpose, they served in the long run as a source of discontent between Bali and Germany. However, the Bali-German allies in 1898 avenged the ignominious German defeat of 1891. Mankon was sacked, and a large number of the youth were taken into labour camps.

The Mankon-Bafut reaction only goes to confirm the fact that the Germans faced Cameroonian resistance in the area. It is probable that if Bali had joined them in fighting the Germans, there would have been greater hopes. But Galega was fully aware of the trend of events in the coastal area where the German colonial forces had been established through the use of force. Galega considered that any resistance could only be temporary with heavier consequences to follow. It was therefore safe to engage in peaceful negotiations rather than resist.

GALEGA I AND GERMAN RECRUITMENT OF LABOUR

Following the German-Mankon-Bafut war, Zintgraff returned to Germany and did not return until 1896. This time, the main objective of the Germans was to recruit labour for the German plantations at the coast. Galega showed reluctance to this but was convinced once more by Zintgraff that it was necessary. Galega felt it was unsafe for his people who might be attacked by the coastal people, but Zintgraff guaranteed their safety. Thus, an agreement was reached for the supply of labour by Galega I.

It will be noted that by the summer of 1896, the Bali-Mundame road started in April 1892, was completed. The movement of labourers to the coast was therefore eased, although it was still achieved through trekking, as no vehicles were yet in use. The export of labourers from the Western Grassfields was all through Bali. It is to be noted that at the receiving end at the coast, the imported labourers from the Grassfields were considered to be Bali. The huge number led to the creation of special quarters for their reception and lodging; hence, to this day, the greatest settlement area for them remains known as the Bali quarter in Douala. As we shall see later, Bali's involvement in the recruitment of labour was going to affect the unity of her empire.

However, in that same year, 1896, Galega I sent for the Basel Mission to extend her influence to Bali. But the mission was not yet ready to expand to the Western area.

In 1901, Galega I died after having successfully established a solid domestic policy and a strong foreign policy. To a large extent, he was the founder of the major institutions that exist today for the day-to-day life of the Bali people. Through him, Western civilisation, through education, missionary activities, and international trade, spread in the Western Grassfields. Thus, Zintgraff's description that he was "the wisest and boldest African leader" he ever met was true.

FONYONGA II: 1901–1940

At his death in 1901, Galega's eldest son, Tita Nji and once possible claimant to the throne through his bravery and leadership as a governor in parts of his father's conquered empire, had died five years earlier, thereby eliminating the possibility of a succession crisis. Tita Gwenjang, who ruled a large part of the empire and had proven very shrewd, courageous and competent through many gains on the battlefields and who had the support of the powerful BaLolo or Ntaiton people led by Tita Fokum, the then most popular and highly respected retainer, became Fonyonga II.

In order to avoid German influence and an eventual clash, he requested the European imperialists to settle outside his own headquarters. Thus, the German headquarters, which had been in Bali from 1894, was transferred to Bamenda in 1901. It is worth noting that this did not lead to any conflict between Bali and the Germans. This can be proved by the fact that Bali still cooperated with the Germans in 1902 when Colonel Pavel undertook punitive expeditions against Mankon and Bafut. Furthermore, he urged the Basel Mission to reconsider the request his father had made almost a decade earlier for the establishment of a school. They sent Ferdinand Ernst and Rudolf Leimbacher, who became the pioneer teachers of Western education in the Western Grassfields. These missionary professional teachers started formal education in Bali in 1903.

In pursuance of his desire to limit his empire from what could be dominated by the Germans, he agreed with the Germans on the list of member states, which Glauning, captain and stationmaster, listed on the 15th of June 1905 as below.

Translation

15th June 1905
To BALI belong the towns of:

1. Babadju
2. Bamessinge
3. Bangang
4. Bapinyi
5. Bamessong
6. Bamowa
7. Baminyi
8. Babessi
9. Babudjang
10. Bambo
11. Bamofa
12. Batebo
13. Bammyensi
14. Bamunung
15. Bamendschong
16. Batabi
17. Bandscha
18. Babosa
19. Fonyam
20. Fobang
21. Take
22. Fongu
23. Bafotscho
24. Baba
25. Bangwa
26. Bafomessang

27. Bambetu
28. Fongwen
29. Banti
30. Fongu (at Babadju)
31. Babundshi

(Sgd) Glauning
Captain & Stationmaster
Bamenda, 15th June 1905

The Germans hoped that by recognising these 31 states, Fonyonga would assist them in recruiting plantation labour from his empire. But, owing to his knowledge of the evil of forced labour and how dwindling it was to his empire, he put up a strong resistance to labour recruitment. He likened labour recruitment to the slave trade and saw in it an attempt to depopulate the empire. This economic factor, more than any other, embittered the German-Bali relations and made them enemies till their departure in 1914.

The Germans paid back by announcing the independence of the 33 states from Bali vassalage. Henceforth, they had to pay their taxes directly to the German administration. Those states that had capitulated to Bali and lost some of their land wanted the German administration to reclaim the land for them. However, the Germans could not go that far due to the disastrous consequences. The idea had, however, been planted, and it was left to the British who replaced the Germans to consider.

Some scholars (Soh, 1981) have seen this list as a German attempt to subjugate those states under Bali paramountcy. They agree, however, that Bali dominated a larger portion of the region before the advent of the Germans, but they fail to recognise the list as part of the Bali empire that was reduced and placed under German tutelage if a careful study of their wars of conquest is considered. Thus, the list of 31 states does not portray Bali at the height of her domination over the true empire. Rather, colonialism may be considered a determining factor in the dissolution of Bali domination in the Western Grassfields.

The German colonial ambition geared towards economic exploitation could not tolerate the existence of such a powerful African kingdom for long. They had to intrigue from time to time with the subject states and force Bali to grant their independence. From 1906, the Germans' desire to recover the 2,000 rifles handed to them by Zintgraff and Bali's refusal to do so raised more suspicions, as the Germans felt threatened in the region. Consequently, from the second half of the first decade, the Germans sought an alternative power and found favour in the Bamum led by King Njoya. German-Bali relations became strained until their departure following their capitulation at World War I. To demonstrate their hatred for Bali, the Germans burnt down the Bali palace during their retreat in 1914, with the hope of destroying the Zintgraff guns and all that had been acquired during the German period. And to indicate their concern for the Bamum, all the Germans in the Western Grassfields withdrew during the early part of the war to Foumban, the Bamum headquarters.

In spite of this strained Bali-German relation during the reign of Fonyonga, it must not be forgotten that Bali gained from the German presence. As the premier seat of education, the early educated people came from Bali. The language was widely written and used in the region as a medium of expression by the educated people of the time. Fonyonga himself took part in recruiting schoolchildren and in sponsoring schools, as well as granting scholarships.

Fonyonga also encouraged long-distance or inter-kingdom trade during the German colonial period. He gave special recognition to enable traders and raised regular taxes in kind and cash. Trade between the Western Grassfields and the southern forest region was through Bali.

There was also a remarkable change in the people's social life. The increasing influence of riches acquired through trade and that of Western culture, promoted not only by trade and education, but also by the Christian religion, produced a more sophisticated lifestyle in Bali, which was copied by many people in the region and attracted many settlers. This explains why Bali Nyonga which originally was one of the smallest of the Balis has become the largest.

The attraction of this new culture and its expansion in the Western Grassfields has been regarded by some scholars as a deliberate German attempt to promote Bali influence. This allegation may be disproven when one considers the increasing number of people volunteering to settle in Bali during the period, eager to enjoy the new splendour of the place. These included about 3000 BaTi people who, after difficult relations with the Bamum and Bansoa, sought a settlement in Bali. Shortly after, a smaller group from the village of Bawock, led by chief Nana, son of Nta-kam, who was fleeing from the hostility of the chief of Bangante, followed. Fonyonga displaced sub-chiefs like Fokinyang and Tita Ndumu in order to settle these strangers who paid regular homage, tributes and taxes to him.

Although the Bawocks' choice of Bali was equally influenced by their relationship with the BaTi, it is clear to note that when the BaTi were forced to leave Bali in 1911 and they took the Bawock with them, they (the Bawock) pleaded through the Basel Missionary Dr Adolf Vielhauer in 1912 that Fonyonga may allow them to return to Bali. Owing to the Fon's goodwill, the Bawock were brought back to settle in Bali. The delegation sent by the Fon to bring back the Bawock people included individuals such as Nji-Mondikam Dingbula, Mamfondikam, and Kungwe. Chief Nana and his people thus returned to Bali, continuing to pay regular tribute to Fonyonga. They were settled in Fomndzu (the area earlier occupied by the BaTi people).

FONYONGA AND WORLD WAR I

Despite the strained relations with Bali, Fonyonga provided the Germans with adequate assistance when the war broke out in 1914. The Fon placed part of his army at the disposal of the Germans. They fought until Mbalmayo (Wurimayo), where many of them stopped and returned to Bali. Many more died while others continued to Rio Muni never to return.

This magnanimity of Fonyonga may be explained by his desire to obey the oath of non-intrigue his father had taken with Zintgraff; a true example of Bali's respect for treaties. It may be necessary to point out that in 1912, when King Bell of Douala wrote to Fonyonga II and Njoya of Bamum that they should join forces to fight against German imperialism, Fonyonga declined but did not betray while Njoya released the information to the Germans who arrested and executed the Douala nationalist. Thus, the Bali rulers remained faithful to the oath.

Meanwhile, the shrewd and astute Fonyonga reserved a befitting welcome for the British army, which did not hesitate to recognise him immediately as the paramount ruler of the region. He had seen the war as a white man's war, although it had damaged his kingdom.

The social and economic life in Bali continued to flourish throughout the war period. His Highness the Fon remained the symbol of power, unity and peace. He maintained what he considered was good of the Germans. For instance, education continued to grow under the able leadership of patriotic teachers like Mr. Lima Gwankudvalla, who later founded a large number of schools in the Western Grassfields. His son, Focho Lima, eventually became the first Cameroonian tutor in the first Cameroonian College, St Joseph College Sasse, when it was opened in 1939 and subsequently became the first Cameroonian to earn an academic degree from a U.S. University in the 1940s. In recognition of the Fon's interest in education, the first British school to be opened in the Grassfields was the Bali Native Authority School in 1922.

Although Christian churches seemed to have died out all over the region due to the departure of missionaries, the church in Bali survived the war, as active Bali Christians continued to preach and gain more followers. Fonyonga allowed freedom of worship and welcomed all religions except those that were considered evil to the social welfare of the people. He did not hesitate after the war to make appeals to the new British colonialists to bring back the missionaries. Thus, on their return, the Basel Mission leaders immediately rushed to Bali to continue the Christian work in the Grassfields. From Bali, Christian faith spread to Mbengwi, Bafut, Bamum and the rest of the Grassfields. Along with it was the spread of schools. Thus, owing to Fonyonga, Bali helped to show the light of development to the entire region.

Economic development included the increasing growth of raffia palms in the valleys, which provided for wine and also for soil conservation. In agriculture, the planting of millet was fast replaced by the planting of maize, an easier plant to cultivate and producing greater yield. The Fon also encouraged the cultivation of tuberous plants alongside cereals.

Like his predecessor, he encouraged long-distance trade. It was common to find Bali traders all over the Bamileke region, beyond Manyu: Victoria, Douala, Ogoja, Onitsha, etc. This increased the wealth of the people and the kingdom.

The trade relations brought many cultural imports. The active trade relations with the Bamileke people introduced a cultural dance called *Laley,* and the forest region trade brought the *Ekpe.* Bali thus became a cultural centre where both the Grassfields and forest people could comfortably settle.

Another phenomenal development in Bali was the growth of a new class. Since the colonial education was geared towards producing administrative assistants, Bali produced a large number of important interpreters and policemen whose prominence left their names on the colonial history. Some of these included the noted interpreter Ayaba, after whom the Bamenda Station hill was called, and today the great Ayaba Hotel has gone to give due respect to his memory. There was also the renowned Major Hannock, who was the first Cameroonian to command the British colonial police force. There was the great chief warder, Maxwell Fohtung and great German commercial clerks who became important traders, such as Mr. Mathew Gwannula alias *Pa 1914* and Mr. Fogam.

It is important to note that Fonyonga continued to work closely with the British administration throughout his reign. This enabled him to supply them enough information about his kingdom which can now serve as useful sources for the cultural and political history of Bali. His personality and shrewdness also reduced the degree of crisis with the neighbouring peoples.

It is therefore possible to close up his reign by saying that he succeeded both in his domestic and foreign policies to maintain the prestige of Bali in the region. He added more oil to the light his ancestors had lit in the Grassfields. The respect to his personality and the splendour of the kingdom lent attraction and envy to the throne. It was therefore not a surprise to the colonial administration that there was a succession crisis following his death in 1940. In any case, the prince's faction, led by Tita Nji (Duga Njingwadnyam), was supported by the British administration to place on the throne an educated, dynamic, and diligent successor, Tita Vincent Samdala. His rival, Tita Nyambi, once more a candidate of the Ntaiton people led by Tita Sama Fokum, lost the throne, even after having received the coronation rites.

VINCENT SAMDALA GALEGA II (1940–1985)

Galega II is the first Bali ruler to be born in the Bali subdivision. He was born in 1906. He took advantage of the educational possibilities then available to go to school. Although the war delayed him, he graduated with the highest certificate of the time in 1924. He then opted for studies in medicine. Like all victims of the colonial system, he was only trained to assist and never given full formal training. This situation helped to increase his hatred of colonial rule, as we shall see later on. However, from 1924 till 1940, when he became the Fon, Prince Samdala assisted the colonial masters in the medical field. It is certain that with the double cultural background (Western and African) and because of the poor treatment of the Africans, an elite like him must have been waiting anxiously for any opportunity to liberate his country from colonialism. It was therefore not surprising when he accepted to take the throne as Galega II

Immediately he got to the throne, he recruited literate assistants into his government including a secretary who recorded all events. Three of his prominent secretaries were Mr. Dook, Mr. Alfred Daiga and Mr. Nteh. He also recruited literate people into the council and some as members of the court. He encouraged most successors to traditional posts to be literate people. All the measures were aimed at strengthening the political structure of Bali and maintaining her eminence in the region. He equally made occasional consultations for necessary advice with well-positioned Bali people in the administration and in the private sector.

He undertook very important economic and social reforms aimed at injecting new impetus into the development of the kingdom. He took advantage of the creation of agricultural extension workers and got them to advise his people. The old two farming season was improved upon. Horse rearing was gradually replaced by cattle. Economic plants such as coffee and eucalyptus were encouraged. Fish ponds were built to encourage fishery. For agriculture to succeed, he found it important to build farm-to-market roads. Roads were built to all villages within the kingdom to facilitate the movement of vehicles for the evacuation of farm products. At first, the building of culverts and bridges posed problems, but his regular appeals for communal labour and people's desire for development led to success. Techniques of farming also underwent a radical change. For example, fertiliser was introduced to improve yield. Oxen farming was also introduced, including some machine farming at the tail end of his reign. Thus, subsistence farming in Bali gave way to cash crop farming. There is no doubt that during Galega's reign, Bali was the granary of the Grassfields region and exported food such as corn, beans, garri, plantains, coffee, pineapples, guava, sugar cane, etc., beyond this region.

The economic transformation obviously introduced social changes of great significance. The numerous bamboo and grass houses were transformed into permanent brick houses with corrugated iron roofs. This saved the people from the seasonal repairs of their houses and the threat of regular fire accidents. They could therefore pass their energies into other productive activities. Galega encouraged adult literacy classes and urged most adults, especially the family heads to attend the classes. Many people finally gained positions of recognition in Bali because of the certificates they obtained from these schools.

With the improved economic position and the acquired riches, the taste for industrialised goods increased, and this elevated the people's living standard. By 1954, Bali was the first kingdom in the region to enjoy pipe borne water, and before the end of Galega's reign, there was electricity in Bali. These basic facilities helped to improve the people's living conditions and to bring in other social services. With the flowing wealth and the cooperation of the dynamic citizens, Galega embarked on the renovation of the palace and the piazza, which were completed in 1960.

In education, Galega like his predecessors, did not relent in efforts to improve its expansion in the kingdom. He took an active part in giving teachers and pupils the basic comfort they required. He shared school buildings and teachers' buildings to individual village chiefs not only to build but to maintain. He regularly reminded his people of the importance of education. He also struggled to bring in more schools, whether with the assistance of the government or with that of the church. When he ascended to the throne in 1940, there were only two primary schools in Bali, with none having a complete cycle. But at his death, there were already 13 full-cycle primary schools. It is significant to note that he took an active part in bringing the first secondary school into this region in 1949, just under a decade after succeeding his father. This was the Basel Mission College, Bali, which since 1957 became known as the Cameroon Protestant College Bali, following an understanding between the Presbyterian Church in Cameroon and the Cameroon Baptist Church. This college has produced very useful elites and development agents not only for Bali or the Western Grassfields but for the entire nation and Africa. He was a permanent member of the board of Governors. Before his death, two more colleges, a Typing Institute and a nursery school, had been established. These schools do not only train Bali children. They train Cameroonians from all over the nation. Thus, although the Bali empire no longer exists, it continues to shine a light in the region.

GALEGA II AND POLITICS

Besides domestic politics, Galega II played a very important role as a nationalist in the struggle for independence. It must be remembered that he came to the throne during the Second World War. This war awakened the spirit of nationalism in many Cameroonians. But for Galega II, it only rekindled his hatred for colonial rule. Thus, while consolidating his throne, he was equally planning for his participation in national liberation after the war.

Like his predecessors, Galega was enjoying the privileges of Indirect Rule. But unlike them, he was planning on how to convert these privileges to national advantage. It was therefore an important opportunity when the Fon, along with Chief Manga Williams of Victoria, were made the first political representatives of Cameroon in the Nigerian Eastern House of Assembly in 1946. Galega II closely worked with the Cameroon elites to present the Cameroon case. This caused repeated changes in the colonial constitution. In 1953, he attended the Mamfe Conference that largely decided the establishment of a regional House of Assembly in Cameroon. In 1957, he attended the Nigerian Constitutional Conference at Lancaster House in London, where he played a crucial role in tilting the political balance in favour of the Reunification Movement led by Dr. John Ngu Foncha.

When he returned from London, he became a strong proponent of Reunification. He convinced most of his contemporaries to get their people to support Reunification. Thus, Bali became one of the strongholds for Reunification in the country. To successfully play his role of guiding the other traditional rulers, Galega presented the need for a Cameroon House of Chiefs. He is undoubtedly the architect of the Southern Cameroons House of Chiefs, an idea he brought back from participating in political affairs in Nigeria (Ndi, 1982). He crowned his efforts by contributing significantly at the Foumban Constitutional Conference in 1960, which led to Reunification and total independence for Cameroon.

The achievement of independence did not fully satisfy Galega. He knew national unity had not yet been achieved. Consequently, he threw his total weight behind the single party when it came and became the pioneer Mezam Section President. Thereafter, he decided to drop politics, having shown in many ways that he loved his country and cherished the freedom of his people. It was not, therefore, an exaggeration when President Paul Biya, on hearing of his death, said, "Fon Galega was a great citizen and militant who performed his duties without reservations and dedicated his life to the service of the nation."

GALEGA II AND THE BALI LAND PROBLEM

One of the major preoccupations of Galega II during his reign was that of frontier dispute. As mentioned earlier, Galega was bound to inherit a colonial problem established by the Germans through their "divide and rule" policy when they incited the member states of the Bali empire to rise for their independence. The uncoordinated dissolution of the empire and the administration's inability to award such states parts of the Bali land led to many different attempts by them to gain the land. At times, they used petitions. At other times, they used force. In all, they failed as the British administration found it not justifiable to carve out conquered lands and give them to the conquered people.

Galega II used educated Bali people, experienced administrators and former police and army officers available in the kingdom to find solutions to the land problems. It must be noted that the climax of this problem was in 1952-1953, when almost all the surrounding neighbours rose in a war against Bali but were repulsed ignominiously. In view of the gravity of the situation, the government decided to submit the problem to a Commission of Inquiry with the hope of finding a lasting solution. After a thorough investigation, the Commission placed the blame on the invaders. A collective fine of ten thousand pounds sterling was imposed on all the people who invaded Bali. (See details in Extraordinary Nigeria Gazette No. 45, Vol. 39 of 20th August 1952 and Extraordinary Nigeria Gazette No. 37, Vol. 40 of 8th June 1953). The wise Fon Galega II did not fail to make a valuable investment with this money. The nine thousand pounds handed to him were placed on the realisation of pipe-borne water.

Galega's success here was very significant. First of all, because henceforth he had a legal backing which reduced further land problems and re-established respect for him and his people. Secondly, because he proved once more that Bali could still maintain and even gain more land through the barrel of the gun. Thirdly, that he and his people were loyal citizens respecting the law and could only go to war for their defence. It should be noted, however, that the British decision not to yield to the neighbours' demand for land was a wise one since that could very easily set a dangerous precedent in the administration of the territory. The rest of the colonial period thus went with no further agitation for land. It was equally the case in the decade and a half that followed independence. But owing to new developments in the political leadership of the nation, when Galega decided to drop from active politics because of ill-health and age, the land issue seemed once more to surface. The ailing Fon, however, did not fail to continue the struggle and point out to the government the consequences of arbitrarily changing land boundaries. Thus, until his death, he maintained intact the territory granted him by conquest and by legal administration in 1952/53.

GALEGA II AND CULTURAL REVIVAL

The cultural revival that accompanied nationalism throughout the country did not fail to attract the attention of Galega II and his people. Upon ascending to the throne, he encouraged numerous cultural activities. The Lela and Voma celebrations became more regular and in greater pomp and pageantry. Other cultural groups, such as Danga, Nchibi/Conicon, Nabionga, Kundu, Nkundung, Mandet, Laley, Ngungang, and Njab-Fotoh, graced many cultural shows.

Different cultural groups were called up regularly in turns to display at public shows and to compete during entertainments. The Fon himself was a member of all cultural groups. He also encouraged the artists by awarding them prizes and other distinctions. This led to the growth of many musicians, wood carvers, dress makers, etc.

He encouraged Bali men and women to dress decently by changing the dress of his own wives. Thus, the "ngwashi" and "tikwan" attire, which predominated the scene when he came to power, disappeared except during ceremonies.

The Fon also tolerated many religions. During his reign, the Catholics gradually found a large following while the Presbyterians continued to grow in numbers. The Muslim religion also became important as some Bali people became converted to it.

GALEGA II AND ADMINISTRATION

The Fon gave the colonial administration all the services required of him and worked so hard as an auxiliary of the government that he was always called upon in major policy matters. As mentioned earlier, he used the good relationship that was established wisely to the advantage of his people without hurting the colonial government.

In the same way, he respected and closely served the national government from its inception after reunification until his death. In recognition of his faithful services and his dynamism in the struggle for independence, his kingdom was granted an administrative status by a Presidential decree in 1966, which made it a district. And in 1979, it was raised to the level of a subdivision. It is obvious that when the administration is brought nearer to the people, the development of the area is accelerated. It is already evident that the opening of many government services in the subdivision is the government's attempt to increase the rhythm of development.

In conclusion, it is not difficult to pass a positive historical judgement on the reign of Galega II. After all, his political, social and economic reforms are clear indications of his hard work and successful reign. He was therefore a wise, diligent and dedicated father of his people. Some critics indeed regard him as an ambitious leader who was more concerned with national affairs than concentrating on the immediate problems of his people. But the preceding pages state clearly that he felt he was naturally called not only to serve Bali but to serve Cameroon as a whole. It is also noted that as a national figure, he could easily solve Bali problems. It is true that in any family, there are problems because of individual differences. Bali could not have been an exception to this natural law, especially when land problems were concerned. Yet Bali showed in their usual concerted manner that they were peacefully united behind their Fon in the search for peace, political, economic, social and cultural developments. This explains why they mourned his death to the recognition of everybody as all heads were shaved, a rare tradition that identified the people with absolute solidarity and true loyalty to their ruler.

The arrival on the throne of a University Lecturer, Dr. Ganyonga III, in obedience to the call of his father and the love of his people and their tradition, is yet another indication of a new era of hope. It is believed that with such a sacrifice, he will be able to marry the latest Western culture with the Bali culture to produce a yet brighter future for Bali.

BIBLIOGRAPHY

Ardener, E. M. (1965). *Historical notes. On the scheduled monuments of West Cameroon*. Buea.

Chilver, E. M. (1961). Nineteenth-century trade in Bamenda Grassfields, Southern Cameroons. *Ubersee, 45*.

Chilver, E. M. (1963). *Native Administration in West Central Cameroon 1902-1954*. London.

Chilver, E. M. (1964). A Bamileke Community in Bali Nyonga: Notes on the Bawock. *African studies, 23*.

Chilver, E. M. (1966). *Zintgraff's exploration in Bamenda, Adamawa and Benue lands 1889-1892*. Buea.

Chilver, E. M. (1967). *Paramountcy and protection in the Cameroons, The Bali and the Germans 1889-1913*. New Haven.

Chilver, E. M., & Kaberry, P. M. (1961). An outline of the traditional system of Bali Nyonga. *Africa, 31*(4).

Chilver, E. M., & Kaberry, P. M. (1967). *Traditional Bamenda: The precolonial History and Ethnography of the Bamenda Grassfields*. Buea.

Conrade. (1972). *Atlas Regional du Cameroun*. Yaounde.

Crowder, M., & Ikime, O. (1972). *West African Chiefs*. Ife University

Press.
Duncan, N. C. (1971). *Bali Area - Cameroons Province.*
Fielding, L. *A brief history of Bali.* Translated by Kalle Njie, Buea.
Fonyuy, F. C. (1973). The concept and exercise of power in a traditional milieu: A Case Study of Bali Nyonga City State. *Science and Technology Review, 3.*
Goodliffe, F. A. *The Bali reorganisation Report.* Buea.
Gwanfogbe, M. B. (1985). *The evolution of Western education in the British Cameroons, 1916-1961* [Unpublished master's thesis]. Ibadan.
Hunt, W. E. (1925). *Assessment Report on the Bali clan in the Bamenda Division of the Cameroons Province.* Buea.
Jeffreys, M. D. W. (1957). The Bali of Bamenda. *African Studies, 16.*
Kaberry, P. M. (1962). Retainers and Royal Households in Cameroons Grassfields. *Cahiers d'Etudes Africaines, 31.*
Kale, P. M. (1967). *Political Evolution in the Cameroons.* Buea.
Kibot, G. (1980). *The Germans in the Bamenda Grassfields 1884-1916.* Yaounde.
Ndangam, A. F., & Nwana, E. M. (1981). *Portrait of their Royal Highnesses.* BACCUDA.
Ndi, A. N. (1983). *Fifty years of the Mill Hill missionaries in West Cameroon 1922-1972.* London.
Ntali, J. B. (1986). *The Exercise of Traditional Authority in Bali Nyonga.* Yaounde.
Obaro, I. (Ed.). (1980). *Groundwork of Nigerian History.* Heinemann.
Rudin, H. (1938). *Germans in Cameroons 1884-1916, A Case Study in modern imperialism.* New Haven.
Soh, P. B. (1978). *A Study of Bali Nyonga History and the Lela Cult.* Yaounde.
Soh, P. B. (1985). *The passing of a great leader, Galega II of Bali Nyonga (1906-1985).* Bamenda.

2

The Biography of V.S. Galega II (1906–1985)

Gwannua Ndangam

Vincent Samdala Galega II, who ruled Bali Nyonga from 1940 to 1985, is considered to have been a great leader (Soh, 1985), and many would subscribe to this view. Opinions, however, would differ as to what precisely it was that made him great. The present account of his life attempts to put together the facts of his life and assess the grounds on which this assertion is justified.

BIRTH AND EARLY LIFE

V.S. Galega II was born in Bali Nyonga in 1906. He acceded to the throne of Bali Nyonga on August 30, 1940, ruled for 45 years, and died on September 18, 1985, at Shishong Hospital in Nso.

The name *Samdala* has led some writers of his biography to imagine that he was a twin.[1] However, he was not a twin, and Samdala is not a traditional name for twins in Bali.[2] His younger sister, Lydia Penvadga, was the only other child of his mother.

1 Soh Bejeng Pius, *The Passing of a Great Leader: Galega II of Bali Nyonga (1906–1985)*. Page 4 and page 11). This minor inaccuracy apart, Bejeng's account of Galega II's life gives interesting details about the public life of Fon V.S. Galega II.

2 Twins in Bali are named Samgwa'a (1st male twin), Samjela (2nd male twin), Nagwa (first female twin), Najela (second female twin). Bejeng's guess that he was a twin is interesting and must be traced to the first

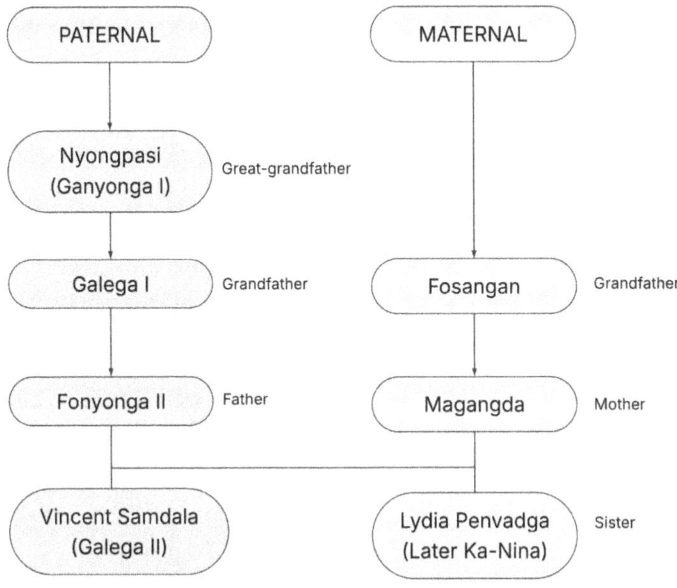

Figure 2.1. Galega II's family line. Also see Appendix I for a full pedigree of his family.

At the age of 10, he started his education at a Roman Catholic religious school in Bali. Education at the time was in a state of flux in the country. In Bali, there were two religious schools: a protestant one under the late Lima Gwankudvalla at the then Basel Mission

morpheme (Sam) of the name. Commonly in Bali tradition, any first child of a newly crowned Fon can be named *Samdala* in the case of a male child) or *Nadala in* the case of a female child) to signify the arrival of such a child, close to the rare *dala* dance which features at the crowning of the reigning Fon. Galega II was given this name at birth not only for this reason but additionally because he happened to have been born on the very day, *Ndasi,* when Doh Ba Moh died. Doh Ba Moh was the grandson of Nyongpasi, and according to Ba Tita Labi, the *dala* dance was supposed to feature at the *death celebration* of Doh Ba Moh in keeping with Bali tradition when mourning important members of the Royal family.

(premises at Tikali and a Roman Catholic one run by Mathias Baina, a catechist who hailed from Nso. This group operated in the first court hall built in 1918 above the palace gate site of the present grandstand).

How long Prince Samdala remained in this school before moving to the next school is not known. What is clear is that Prince Samdala's early life swung like the pendulum of a wall clock between two genuine believers in education. At home, his father, Fonyonga II, was a great promoter of education. The Fon himself was not literate, but he promptly recognised the benefits of formal education when the Germans introduced it in Bali in 1903. He ordered children to be sent to school, and he himself played the role of an Inspector, visiting the school regularly and personally punishing all cases of truancy and absenteeism reported to him. Frequently, a pupil and his father were both punished by Fonyonga II for a child's disobedience or absence from school.

On the other hand, the Fon generously used his own private resources to support school work. He paid fees for all the children in the entire school for two months in 1924 before fees were finally abolished.

Hunt mentions in his *Assessment Report* that Fonyonga II sent "more than one son as far as Calabar for schooling." It is very unlikely that Prince Samdala was one of these children who went to Calabar. Ba Lima Gwankudvalla recruited and sent three young men to Calabar for further schooling and training as teachers. The plan was for these young men to return and teach in the new school in Bali. It is likely that the sons referred to by Hunt were these three young men rather than any particular sons of the Fon.

In school, the life of Prince Samdala was greatly dominated by that pioneer schoolmaster, the late Ba Lima Gwankudvalla, whose interest and efforts to foster education led him to start several schools and to carry the future Fon from one school to another. Ba Lima Gwankudvalla was a man of great personal initiative. He was a teacher under the Germans and had been captured along with Rev. Vielhauer as war prisoners by the British, but later on released on the condition that they did not spy for the Germans. The moment he was set free[3] he returned to schoolwork. He travelled to Fumban and received a private intensive English course for eight months under an English lady missionary.

Upon returning to Bali, he started a secular-oriented school (circa 1920). His school became popular, absorbing practically all the children from the existing missionary schools, including Prince Samdala, whom he personally assisted with writing materials bought from Calabar. The schoolmaster took a special interest in the schoolwork of the young Prince and became like a "father"[4] to him.

While on a visit to Bali the early British administrator in Bamenda, Hunt, was surprised to discover an organised English medium school flourishing where British men had established none. The British administrator was particularly delighted to be greeted by the children in English. He discussed with Ba Lima Gwankudvalla the possibility of the government coming to his assistance and the need (in that event) of moving the school out of the Mission compound to more suitable premises. Ba Gwankudvalla proposed Bamenda Station as being more central and suitable to serve the other villages of the Bamenda area.

Hunt accepted the proposal, and Ba Gwankudvalla was himself subjected to an examination to ascertain his level of education and suitability as a teacher. He performed well in the examination and was consequently appointed in 1922 to open the Bamenda government school. To this school, he decided to take along all the children from his school, including Prince Samdala. These children from

3 After receiving some strokes of the cane.

4 This foreshadowed a future relationship for Ba Francis Elias Lima Gwankudvalla, who later on became the father-in-law of Fon V.S. Galega II when the latter married Na-Kega, the former's daughter. From this marriage was to come the future Fon Ganyonga III.

Bali formed the nucleus of the Bamenda government school when it opened at the present Bamenda Government Residential Area.

Figure 2.2. Ba Francis Elias Lima Gwankudvalla, pioneer school master and educator in the North West Province.

One year later, Ba Gwankudvalla was posted back to Bali to formally open the Bali Native Authority school, and he left Prince Samdala to continue his education in Bamenda. The young prince took an active part in all school activities, distinguishing himself in games and sports. He played football well and was a frequent winner in long races. These physical activities toughened him, and in 1928, when he had to undertake his longest trek, he accomplished this with no difficulty. The journey took him to Njinikom, where he was baptised into the Roman Catholic faith by Rev. Father Jacob.

Because of the acute need for educated young people in the various Public Services at the time, Standard Five was considered adequate to start work. Consequently, Prince Samdala left school in 1924, after completing Standard Five. In the same batch graduating with him from government school Bamenda was his half-brother Tita James Dinga.

MEDICAL PROFESSION

On leaving school, he joined the medical department and trained as a nurse at the Bamenda General Hospital (located then where the present Magistrate's Court in Bamenda is). During the period of his training, he got married to his first wife, Ma Duga.

Upon completing his training, he was posted to open a Dispensary at Ndop. While serving at Ndop, his father arranged for him to take additional wives. Among those who joined him at Ndop were Nafog Na-Manyi, Na Feh, and Ma-Godsabi. From Ndop, he was transferred to Batibo Dispensary, where he served for some time before moving to Bali Dispensary at his father's proposal, whose health was failing.

ACCESSION TO THE THRONE

The late Fonyonga II made his selection for a successor known only to very close associates, but the Fon's very generous attitude towards Prince Samdala, especially in the many wives he sent to the prince while the latter was dispensary attendant at Ndop and Batibo, made it obvious that this was the future Fon in the making.

As his health deteriorated, Fonyonga II contacted Dr. Jeffreys, the then Resident at Bamenda, and pleaded for Prince Samdala to be transferred to the Bali dispensary. The reason given to the Resident for this plea was that the Fon needed someone he had confidence in to take care of his health while working in the dispensary in Bali. But the prudent Fonyonga II wanted in fact to remove the obstacle of distance between the throne and the heir to it. Apparently, the Fon sensed the cloud of rivalry gathering between Prince Samdala and his first son, Tita Nyambi, who was supported by Tita Sama Fokum.

Figure 2.3. Fon V.S. Galega II in his court after he ascended the throne of Bali Nyonga

In spite of this precaution, Prince Samdala did not get it smooth getting to the throne. Before he learnt of his father's death, Tita Nyambi (his half-brother) was already in the palace, and the news of the Fon's death and the succession of Tita Nyambi had been communicated to the Resident in Bamenda. But other members of the Royal family, faithful to the will of the late Fon, quickly assembled at the house of Tita Nji near the palace and sent for Prince Samdala. The group led by Tita Nji marched into the palace, supported by a powerful armed wing of the Kundu[5] Association.

5 One of the associations in Bali where the men meet weekly for drinking and discussing matters of mutual interest. The association was based at the Njenka quarter that is distinguished by this name.

This armed wing surrounded the palace determined to ensure the succession of Samdala and to defend him against any rivalry faction. Meanwhile, Tita Nji's group and Prince Samdala's supporters marched into the palace and ousted Tita Nyambi, who fled from Bali, leaving the throne to Prince Samdala, who was crowned as Galega II on the 30th of August 1940.

HIS RULE (1940–1985)

His accession to the throne turned out to be widely acclaimed in Bali and there was popular rejoicing for months afterwards.

The idea of development appears to have been uppermost in the new Fon's mind as seen by the fact that a few months after his accession to the throne, he organised the Bali Development Committee in 1941 to plan streets for Bali town and to open up roads in the area. Two years later, in 1943, he founded the Bali Improvement Union (BIU) to foster the education of capable young people. This organisation launched a scholarship scheme from which many young people were able to pursue higher education abroad in Europe and the U.S.

In the mid-40s, V.S. Galega II became the Chairman of the Bali Area Rural Council. When later on, the Gah of Bali Gham assisted him as Vice-Chairman of the Bali Council, the idea of an association for the Chamba family occurred to him. He contacted the other Chamba Fons in the North-West Province and the *Chamba Wat-Coon*[6] was formed to preserve the rich cultural heritage of Bali Chamba. The five Fons of the Chamba group met frequently and exchanged visits, especially during the *Lela* festival.

Although discontent from some of the minority groups[7] simmered from time to time, internally the reign of Galega II

6 Pan Chamba Association. This group brought together the five Chamba groups: Bali Nyonga, Bali Kumbat, Bali Gham, Bali Gaso and Bali Gangsin.

7 Bawock and Bossa notably.

established peace and cohesion within Bali and made for the development, which is discussed in a separate chapter in this work. Consequently, he had no major question to deal with internally throughout his 45-year rule. Yet from beginning to end, his reign was bedevilled by turmoil and turbulence over land matters with neighbouring villages.

The first decade of his reign witnessed an all-out struggle by villages neighbouring Bali pressing for Bali land to be given to them. Originally, these villages wanted *all* the land occupied by Bali. When this demand appeared ridiculous, the demand later on took the form of asking for the alteration of the Bali boundary to add more land to them. They used all possible channels to press for their demand. First, by a series of petitions, they asked the British administration to give them back the lands they originally occupied before they were conquered by the Balis. The British administration refused to do so. Next, they tried the legal process. The courts ruled against them.

Finally, the villages tried to get back the land by force. In a concerted action in 1952, the villages that surround Bali planned a surprise attack on Bali on all fronts at the same time on the same day. The situation seemed to have tickled that "military preparedness" which Hunt, the British administrator, described as a distinguishing characteristic of the Bali people. V.S. Galega II promptly worked out a defence strategy. His strategy was simple and based on the farming pattern[8] of the Bali population. He ordered all his fighting men to report at their farms, assemble themselves there into fighting contingents and face outwards. He himself took up the best possible position to command: the centre. He stayed in Bali town itself and selected a group of ex-service policemen and

8 Farmlands surround the periphery of Bali boundaries, "as though they stand guard against encroachment by the surrounding villages," (F.A. Goodliffe. D.O. *Bali Reorganisation Report)*.

soldiers who were to be used as reinforcement on any front where reinforcement was needed.

He used this group only once on the Northern front, where the leader of the invading group was killed within the first few shots, and the invaders were repulsed. Brief as it was, this decisive battle marked the turning point of the war, and Bali pressed on their defence, clearing pockets of resistance until the invaders were pushed beyond Bali's boundary on all fronts.

Apart from keeping a standby group for reinforcement during the war, Galega II organised the security of Bali town itself by setting up a network of sentries to guard all entries into Bali at night. He personally supervised this network of sentries riding on a horse and accompanied by a valet *(ntsinted).*

After the disturbances, the colonial government submitted the whole matter to a Commission of Inquiry. After a thorough investigation, the Commission of Inquiry attributed the disturbances to the Widikum tribes. A collective fine of ten thousand pounds sterling was imposed by the government on all the villages involved in the disturbance. Of this sum, nine thousand was passed on to the Balis as compensation.[9]

In 1953, the government also decided to probe the root cause of the war. A commission headed by Justice A.G.B. Manson was appointed to look into the land dispute between Bali and its neighbours. According to this commission, Bali had acquired its land by right of conquest, and the land could not be returned to the original owners.

But the whole land problem that so much occupied his time and energy was not of Galega's own making. It was a problem that had spilt into his hands from his father's reign.

9 The details of this Commission of Inquiry are found in official Gazettes of the time, notably Extra-Ordinary Nigeria Gazette No. 45 Vol. 39 of 20th August 1952 and Extra-Ordinary Nigeria Gazette No. 37 Vol. 40 of 8th June 1963.

Conquered villages even as far back as Galega I had been treated with surprising generosity. As long as they accepted Bali suzerainty over them and demonstrated this in the payment of tribute, they were left as a unit on their land, and a Bali "Tadmanji" was appointed as a liaison between them and Bali on matters of tribute. This policy was likely to achieve rapid pacification as long as Bali maintained its grip on its empire; but the possibility of a future revolt was inherent in the arrangement, and came to the surface in the wake of the strained relations between the Germans and the Balis during the reign of Fonyonga II.

The German Administration had seen in Fonyonga II a powerful ruler whose influence and Empire could be exploited to foster German economic interest. The Germans recognised him as paramount Fon over thirty-three villages outside Bali itself. This added nothing new to the Fon. It merely endorsed what Bali had acquired by conquest before the Germans came, but the aim of the Germans was to use a powerful ruler to secure the recruitment of plantation labourers from the area and the levy of poll tax. This placed Fonyonga II in a rather difficult situation since recruiting people for labour could only be done by the use of force and taxes were not something people paid with a smile. Thus, the actual implementation of these policies by the Fon of Bali nursed resentment by the subordinate villages. The use of force inevitably increased tension between Bali and these villages.

Fonyonga II himself resented being used in this way by the Germans and wanted to maintain peaceful relations with his conquered subjects. He believed that, left on his own, even after all that had happened previously, he could soothe all the ruffled feelings engendered by his uncomfortable middleman role to foster colonial interests.

He finally refused to recruit labourers for the Germans from these subordinate villages. German reaction was swift and direct. They called a meeting in Bamenda and announced to all the villages subordinate to Bali that their vassalage had come to an end and they were free of Bali suzerainty. Thenceforth they were to pay their taxes directly to the administration. Naturally, these villages wanted to see if they could get more than was offered to them. If vassalage was over, could they also be given back their conquered lands? But the Germans would not go that far.

Convinced that it was a question of time and continued persuasion, these villages kept pressing for Bali land to be returned to them even after the Germans left and Fonyonga II died. It was left to the British administration and Galega II to meet the demands of these villages for Bali land to be returned to them. V.S. Galega II fought against the alteration of Bali boundary down to the day he went down to his grave, but the fortunes of the Bali people had changed and the National Government in decree No. 77/525 of 23rd December 1977 did concede to alter the Bali boundary and let natives of neighbouring villages settle on certain areas of Bali land provided this did not involve dislodging previous settlers of Bali origin who chose to stay.

POLITICAL CONTRIBUTION

V.S. Galega II was not a politician, and he himself emphasised this point at several political conferences where he represented traditional rulers. Yet any account of his life that overlooks his role in the political development of Southern Cameroons in particular and the Republic of Cameroon as a whole would be grossly incomplete.

The history of pre-independence Southern Cameroons—as the anglophone provinces of Cameroon were known then—is intimately linked to that of Nigeria. Southern Cameroons was administered as part of Nigeria.

The vital role that chiefs and Fons as traditional rulers could -and did play in political affairs and public administration within Nigeria was recognised as early as 1900 by the first British Governor General of Nigeria, Lord Lugard, who worked out the classical administrative system known as *Indirect Rule*. Indirect Rule for the British colonial officials meant that local affairs would be conducted through indigenous authorities, who had traditional authority over their people instead of directly by them who were foreigners.

The first significant landmark in the constitutional development of Nigeria and the Southern Cameroons appeared in the late 40s with the Richard's Constitution which came into effect in January 1947. This constitution enlarged the legislative Assembly in Nigeria and created Regional Houses of Assembly for each of the three Regions of Nigeria. Southern Cameroons gained nothing by this constitution. It was not recognised as a separate entity but was lumped together as part of Eastern Nigeria. Galega II and Chief Manga Williams of Victoria represented the Southern Cameroons at the Eastern House of Assembly at Enugu. The two were not elected representatives but were part of the eighteen "unofficial" members nominated by the British Administration. As representatives, the two provided political leadership, influencing the direction in which events should take. When, for example, the Cameroon Council met in 1949 in Victoria to press for a separate regional status for Southern Cameroons, it did so under their leadership with Chief Manga Williams acting as Chairman. By the late 50s, when this full Regional status was granted, Chief Manga Williams had retired from active public life, leaving V.S. Galega II to press on for a bicameral legislature for Southern Cameroons with the House of chiefs serving as a second chamber—an idea which V.S. Galega II conceived during his days as a representative in Nigeria.

The Macpherson Constitution, introduced in 1951, introduced elected representatives in both the Regional Houses and the House of Representatives. The election that followed was conducted nationwide, along party lines, and future political leaders[10] of the Southern Cameroons began to emerge.

Figure 2.4. HRH Galega II in front of the Eastern House of Assembly, Enugu, Nigeria.

These leaders promptly realised the need for them to reach the masses through influential traditional authorities. Dr. Endeley, in particular, being the son of a Bakweri chief, realised his need for support from natural rulers. He sought and obtained the full support of V.S. Galega II and other Fons and chiefs. In return, Dr. Endeley supported the demands of the natural rulers for a House of Chiefs while he was leader of Government Business. Up

10 Men like Dr. E.M.L. Endeley, Dibonge, Mbile, S.A. George, Rev. J.C. Kangsen, J. Ndze, etc.

until 1957, Dr. Endeley's party and government had the support of V.S. Galega II, and Bali was a KNC stronghold. But Endeley's relation with the Fon of Bali was shattered rather dramatically at the 1957 constitutional conference in London. The background to the disagreement is traced briefly because it illustrates Galega II's commitment to what he believed was the common good.

The 1957 Constitutional Conference in London (which prepared Nigeria for independence) was preceded in Southern Cameroons by the Bamenda summit conference of May/June 1956 held at the Bamenda Community Hall. The conference brought together all shades of political opinion in Southern Cameroons to prepare for the impending London Conference. Before the Bamenda conference, the delegates generally agreed on the question of greater autonomy for Southern Cameroons, but there was no real consensus on the future of the territory itself after independence. Yet this was the crucial question to he discussed at the coming London conference as far as Southern Cameroons was concerned.

By the time of the Bamenda Summit conference, the Southern Cameroons Delegation to the London conference had already been selected. Southern Cameroons had eight places, and this had been divided between the existing political parties as follows:[11] KNC (4), KNDP (2), KPP (2).

The traditional rulers gathered at Bamenda for the summit were surprised that their group was completely left out of the delegation. They made it clear to the politicians that they would not feel bound by any decision arrived at in London if they were not represented. It was a threat to be taken seriously by the politicians in general and by Dr. Endeley's government in particular. Dr. Endeley promptly cancelled one member of his party's delegation and offered the place

11 KNC was the government party and KNDP was the opposition. KPP obviously had more than their political strength warranted, but by this time, both KNC and KPP had a common policy over the question of continued association with Nigeria.

to the representative of the natural rulers. The natural rulers then elected V.S. Galega II as their representative to London. The official representation to the conference from the Southern Cameroons then stood as follows:

KAMERUN NATIONAL CONGRESS
Dr. E.M.L. Endeley
Fon V.S. Galega II
Mr. J.T. Ndze
Mr. V.E. Mukete (adviser)
KAMERUN NATIONAL DEMOCRATIC PARTY
Mr. J.N. Foncha
Mr. A.N. Jua (adviser)
KAMERUN PEOPLES PARTY
Mr. P.M. Kale
Mr. N.N. Mbile (adviser)

By including Fon Galega II on his official delegation, Dr. Endeley anticipated a reciprocal stand on the part of the natural rulers. He naturally expected them to toe his party line at the conference. It was not an unreasonable expectation since the Fon of Bali, in particular, and the chiefs in general, had up till then always supported the KNC government. Yet on this particular instance, it turned out to be a gross miscalculation.

The natural rulers on their part accepted the place offered to them "as of right,"[12] especially as natural rulers from other Regions of Nigeria were on several official delegations. Furthermore, the natural rulers decided that they were not a political party, and as such, they would express an independent opinion at the conference.

12 Petition by V.S. Galega II dated 6th August 1958 to the High Commissioner for the Southern Cameroons, Lagos. In this petition, V.S. Galega II insisted that he went to London as a representative of the Natural Rulers and not as a member of the KNC delegation.

They went ahead on their own and prepared a separate memorandum which was signed by Fon Achirimbi II of Bafut, who was the chairman of the chiefs' conference, and by V.S. Galega II (as Delegate to the Conference).

In London, three memos[13] were presented by the Southern Cameroons delegation stating different viewpoints on the important question of the future of Southern Cameroons after Nigeria became independent.

The memo by the KNC opted for Southern Cameroons to remain part of Nigeria.

> It is the wish of the people of the Southern Cameroons delegates to this Conference, that the Southern Cameroons should cease to be a Quasi-Federal Territory, and be granted FULL TERRITORIAL AUTONOMY forthwith, its own Governor, and the necessary political and administrative machinery, and in accordance with the terms of the United Nations Trusteeship Agreement.
>
> We are agreed that an autonomous Cameroons territory remains in association with the Federation of Nigeria as at present, but in accordance with the provisions of the United Nations Charter, it will be necessary for Her Majesty's Government to review the 'Trust Territory's Association with Nigeria before She attains independence.[14]

The KNDP asked for secession:

13 One presented by the KNC/KPP, one by the KNDP and one by the Fon of Bali V.S. Galega II.

14 "Memorandum presented jointly by the Kamerun National Congress, the Kamerun People's Party and the Fon of Bali to the Nigeria Constitutional Conference, May/June 1957."

Since the Cameroons and Nigeria were brought under one Central Government many things which will be remembered in favour or against have happened. It will be recalled that this joint administration was arranged purely by the British Government for its Own convenience, and that neither Nigerians nor Cameroonians knew what was happening in those days. Now that Cameroonians have been given the opportunity to say what relations they choose to have with Nigeria, they should be free to do so in order that they alone should be responsible for any decision they will take. The KNDP will repulse any insinuation from the Nigerian Delegates which will induce the Cameroons delegates to act contrary to the best interest of our people:

It should, however, be noted that a friendly atmosphere has been created between Nigerians and Cameroonians as they have had to share the same educational institutions and the same Civil Service and amenities. On the other hand, the joint administration has shown a marked neglect of the development of the Cameroons, a fact which has never been disputed by even the most sceptic visitor.

The result has been disparity in progress in almost all spheres of life. This has caused a wide awakening in the minds of Cameroonians and the current trend of thought is to manage the affairs of the people in the Cameroons directly under Her Majesty's Government.

Following the present opinion and political movements in Nigeria, the only just course open to Cameroonians is to secede from the Federation and assume direct management of their affairs.[15]

The memo by the Fon of Bali on behalf of the natural rulers came out in favour of separation from Nigeria.

> It is our desire that the Southern Cameroons be granted a full Regional Status with its own Governor ... for its government as quasi-Territory for the last three years had been a great success; that after the Independence of the Federation of Nigeria, the Southern Cameroons shall be the direct responsibility of the Colonial Government.[16]

The memo also came out in support of reunification but stated what all the pro-unification campaigners at the time wanted, i.e. that the two parts of Cameroon should first obtain their separate independence before negotiating for reunification. It was believed that this would give Southern Cameroons a stronger negotiating position at reunification.

Thus, this memo supported the views of Foncha's KNDP and differed markedly from the stance of the KNC. But the embarrassment for Dr. Endeley was not only the fact that the Fon of Bali had refused to toe his party line on a crucial question, it was that the memo presented by him (Dr. Endeley) on behalf of the KNC and advocating integration with Nigeria was said to be a joint memo. It was titled:

> MEMORANDUM PRESENTED JOINTLY BY THE KAMEROUN NATIONAL CONGRESS, THE KAMERUN PEOPLES' PARTY AND THE FON OF

15 "Memorandum presented by the Kamerun National Democratic Party on the Review of the Nigerian Constitution on 23rd May 1957."

16 Chiefs' Conference of the Southern Cameroons: Memorandum to the London Conference.

BALI TO THE NIGERIA CONSTITUTIONAL CONFERENCE MAY/JUNE 1957.

What was more? The memo carried in Appendix B a copy of another memo presented earlier at the Bamenda Summit Conference by the Chiefs' Conference. This memo stated in paragraph 2:

> although the position of the Southern Cameroons in relation to the Federation of Nigeria is a peculiar one, we feel that this territory should for obvious reasons remain within the Federation.

It was, thus, a complete embarrassment for Dr. Endeley that while he claimed that he, the Fon of Bali and the Chiefs' Conference in Southern Cameroons, were unanimous about integration with Nigeria, the Fon of Bali was proposing secession and reunification. The Fon of Bali and Fon Achirimbi II of Bafut had discreetly kept all the politicians ignorant of their stand on the question of association with Nigeria as well as their strategy by which their views would be stated by the Fon of Bali in London and—if necessary— confirmed by a telegram from the Fon of Bafut back home.

The outcome of all these was the sharp disagreement that erupted between Dr. Endeley and the Fon of Bali on the one hand and a pleasant surprise for Dr. Foncha, champion of secession and reunification on the other hand. The Fon of Bali sent a telegram home to the Fon of Bafut to contact all the chiefs and Fons to support Foncha and reunification in advance of his return home. On arrival from London, he himself toured the length and breadth of Southern Cameroons, convincing the natural rulers to throw their weight in support of reunification and Foncha's KNDP. He informed the natural rulers of the package brought from London for them. Southern Cameroons was to have a House of Chiefs within a full Regional setting.

The departure of V.S. Galega II from Dr. Endeley's KNC to support the KNDP and the secession movement posed a serious threat to Dr. Endeley and his government. Dr. Endeley was well aware of the influence of the Fon of Bali among the natural rulers, If, however, he could get members of the proposed House of Chiefs to be grateful to him for the establishment of the House of Chiefs, the Fon of Bali would be isolated and left harmless, But Foncha and the Fon of Bali moved swiftly to foil these plans. Thereupon, Dr. Endeley changed his attitude to the whole question of the natural rulers and their role in political affairs. Willard R. Johnson (1970) puts it succinctly:

> After the defection from his party of the important Fon of Bali, Endeley sought to recapture the support of chiefs (the Fon had systematically set about organizing all of them against Endeley) by begging the administration to establish the House of Chiefs ahead of schedule and before the elections so that he could take credit for the innovation. This ultimately made matters worse, because Foncha, suspecting the motives for this move, claimed Endeley intended to interfere in the Chiefs' affairs by putting his own stooges into the House, or would use the promise of a position in it to pressure the chiefs. The Fon of Bali, aided by Foncha, assembled most of the country's chiefs at Kumba, where they formally rejected the idea of inaugurating the House of Chiefs before the elections.
>
> As the Fon of Bali stepped up his campaign to organize the chiefs against Endeley's KNC, Endeley shifted his position on the role of chiefs and traditionalism in politics. He stated in May 1958, shortly after being installed as prime minister, that, 'we shall also expect

> that in their own interest chiefs and traditional rulers must keep clear of party politics ... Any chief who persists, despite this timely advice, to participate in party politics does so at his own risk' (Johnson, 1970).

Although the warning here was addressed in general terms to all chiefs it was intended primarily for the Fon of Bali. The KNDP leaders exploited the statement and situation to their advantage.

> Foncha and Augustine Jua moved quickly to consolidate the opposition of the grassfields chiefs to Endeley. They proclaimed that the KNC had no regard for "natural rulers," that Endeley was full of hatred for the Bali people, particularly and grassfielders generally (Johnson, 1970).

Meanwhile, by this time arrangements were well underway for a resumption of the constitutional talks in London and Dr. Endeley announced the replacement of the Fon of Bali by the Fon of Bum on the official delegation to the resumed talks. What however could not be taken away from V.S. Galega II was his membership of the Chiefs' conference.

The Chiefs' Conference continued to meet from time to time at different Divisional Headquarters. V.S. Galega II and Achirimbi II of Bafut assumed leadership of the group and became the spokesmen of their colleagues. The influential position of Galega II among his colleagues is obvious from the fact that his two private secretaries, W.T. Dook and A.W. Daiga, successively and concurrently served as secretaries to the Chiefs' conference. The latter's eventual election into parliament on the KNDP platform marked the complete replacement of the KNC influence in Bali by the KNDP.

The Chiefs' conference was the forerunner of the Southern Cameroons House of Chiefs, which was granted at the London constitutional conference. At the inception of the House of Chiefs in Buea, leadership again devolved upon V.S. Galega II and Achirimbi II of Bafut, the two alternating as either Chairman or Vice-Chairman. There was an excellent personal relationship between the two Fons throughout their lives, and their alternating roles in the House of Chiefs never engendered rivalry. They frequently visited each other's palace, even spending nights there. Another dimension to the special relationship of the Fon of Bali and the Fon of Bafut came from the recognition of the four traditional kingdoms of the North-West Province by the House of Chiefs, which accorded the Fon of Bali, the Fon of Bafut, the Fon of Nso and the Fon of Kom special status among the natural rulers. They fell into a special leading class of their own.

Fon V.S. Galega II and Achirimbi II gave Foncha their full support and assisted the KNDP party to win the 1959 general elections. KNDP fought the election on the very question of separation from Nigeria—a question that had thrown the Fon of Bali and Dr. Endeley apart in London. The election of the KNDP confirmed the views of V.S. Galega II and brought J.N. Foncha into leadership in Southern Cameroons.

Shortly after the 1959 elections, the Southern Cameroons political leaders were at the United Nations where they decided on a plebiscite to be conducted asking the people of Southern Cameroons to join either Nigeria or the Republic of Cameroon on achieving independence. Galega II came out in full support of reunification and campaigned vigorously for it. Bali became the stronghold of the movement for reunification.

Meanwhile, the memo presented earlier at the London Constitutional conference by J.N. Foncha on behalf of the KNDP had—among other things—requested separate discussions with the Colonial Secretary. But at the time of this request KNDP was the official opposition and was speaking from a weak position for negotiation. After they won the election, and shortly after returning from the UN, it was time to move to London and talk with British authorities. In November 1960, V.S. Galega II was in the powerful delegation that left for London to discuss exclusively Cameroonian matters. The position of the two natural rulers on the delegation was kept clear this time. V.S. Galega II and Chief Oben were representing the natural rulers and not any political party. The delegation comprised:

Mr. J.N. Foncha, M.H.A. Premier
Mr. A.N. Jua, M.H.A.
Mr. S.T. Muna, M.H.A.
Mr. W.H.O. Effiom, M.H.A.
Dr. E.M.L. Endeley, M.H.A.
Mr. P.N. Motomby Woleta, M.H.A.
Mr. S.E. Ncha, M.H.A.
Rev. J.C. Kangsen
Mr. P.M. Kale, President, Kamerun United Party
The Fon of Bali (Galega II)
Chief Oben

In a brief but eloquent speech at the talks, V.S. Galega II clarified the position of traditional rulers in political matters. In its overtones, the speech seems to have been conceived as a reply to Dr. Endeley's warning to him in 1958.

> "We the natural rulers," he said, "as fathers and traditional Governors of our people are not interested in party politics and political party leadership. But as far as the fate of our country, our people and ours is concerned, we owe a duty to God and posterity to perform.
>
> ... We are fair and impartial. We are neutral in party politics. We are the fathers of all our people, regardless

> of their political affiliations. If our views fall in line with those of any group or groups of politicians, it is purely a matter of natural coincidence based on what is good for the masses of the people.[17]

Back from London, V.S. Galega threw the whole of his traditional weight in campaigning for Reunification and convincing his other colleagues, the Fons and chiefs. The plebiscite, which decided the destiny of Southern Cameroons on February 11th, 1961, resulted in a decision to achieve Independence by joining the Republic of Cameroon

The plebiscite over, the Southern Cameroons leaders, led by Dr. Foncha, began negotiations for reunification. V.S. Galega II attended both the 1961 Bamenda Conference, which worked out a loose federal structure as a basis for reunification, and the Fumban Constitutional conference, which drew up a constitution for the Federal Republic of Cameroon. Here again, the role played by V.S. Galega was just as crucial to the destiny of Southern Cameroons as at Lancaster House in 1957. He prevented a split in the KNDP delegation to the conference, which would have led to the formation of another party. The Southern Cameroons delegation at the conference had advocated a loose federation with Southern Cameroons controlling internal affairs, but Ahidjo wanted a strong central government. As Eyongetah puts it.

> The conference passed over in silence most of the proposals of the Bamenda Conference and the Southern Cameroons delegates found it necessary to devote their energies to salvaging a few of their main points. On the whole, the basic proposals which reflected Southern Cameroons' desire to retain certain political

17 Speech by V.S. Galega II at the Conference.

prerogatives over the states were ignored or overruled.[18]

Among the Southern Cameroons delegation, there were a few who felt that reunification had failed before it even started. Prominent among these was the late Bobe Augustine Ngom Jua, who pleaded with the Fon of Bali to give him (Jua) his blessings to form a new party. Not only did V.S. Galega II refuse, but he also persuaded Jua to stand firmly behind Dr. Foncha and continue the negotiation. The Fumban Conference finally agreed on the Federal Constitution, which ushered in the reunification of Southern Cameroons and the Republic of Cameroon, the two states becoming West Cameroon and East Cameroon, respectively.

Reunification achieved, V.S. Galega II turned his attention and energy to buttress what he had fought for. He rallied the Bali people around the idea of a national party as soon as the idea was clearly presented to him. He himself was elected to head the first Mezam Section of the then CNU at the inception of the party. As the Party's first Section President for Mezam, he attended the first National Congress of the CNU party in Garoua. But as his health waned and age crawled in, he gave up the Mezam section leadership to Fon. S.A. Angwafor III and remained the Sub-Section president of the party in Bali Subdivision until his death in 1985.

PRIVATE LIFE

Although the Bali ascribe to the Fon qualities that place him outside ordinary human[19] the Fon is indeed a human being with a private world. His private world, however, reveals an ordinary human being with extraordinary responsibilities and obligations. V.S. Galega II was married to 35 wives and had over 200 children. He was thus the head of the largest family unit in Bali. The demands

18 Eyongetah T. et al. *A History of the Cameroon.*

19 See *Aspect of Palace Language.*

on him as family head were just as great as his responsibility in public life.

To his wives, he insisted on three things: the first, based on economic considerations, was that they should learn a traditional craft appropriate to women and keep themselves busy. Most of his wives learnt how to weave grass trays *(Kukad).* Secondly, he insisted on their keeping themselves and their premises clean, an idea, no doubt, ingrained in his lifestyle from his medical profession. Thirdly, he got all his wives actively engaged in the learning of the Bali culture. He organised cultural classes for his wives and children and got experts like Tita Labi to teach them *Mubako,* the original language of the Balis, as well as the *Lela* songs and dance. These private classes clearly yielded positive fruits, as could be seen by the role played by the Fon's wives at *Lela* dances, especially in the production of *Lela* music.

FIRE IS EXTINGUISHED

On 18th September 1985, V.S. Galega II died at Shisong hospital in Bui Division. His body was conveyed to Bali the same night he died, and the population of Bali woke up the next morning to hear that the Fon was no more. He had bowed to death as thousands before him (even great ones) had in their turn bowed. For, as Henry Wadsworth Longfellow wrote:

> There is no flock, however watched and tended,
> But one dead lamb is there!
> There is no fireside, howsoe'er defended,
> But has one vacant chair! ....
> We see but dimly through the mists and
> Amid these earthly damps
> What seems to us but sad, funeral tapers
> May be heaven's distant lamps.

J.G. Saxe's six blind men of Hindustan disputed "loud and long" about the elephant they went to see, and that interesting poem leaves us with the impression that the six men never reached a consensus about what an elephant looks like. Yet there was one thing on which all six men were on a "Common ground." They were all talking about *an elephant.* As far as the life of Galega II is concerned, many would stand on the "Common ground" that he was a great Fon. And what made him great? To some, it would he his rule as Fon, which brought unity and development to Bali Subdivision. To others, it would be the "detached" and "disinterested" manner in which he participated in political affairs. In all his political activities, no personal ambition for political gains or posts ever surfaced. To still others, it would be his qualities of justice and forthrightness—sparkling qualities that made many admire him. The greatness of Fon Galega II came, no doubt, from all these and perhaps more. It is our view that while several things contributed to making Galega II admirable and great, his greatness rests solidly on two fundamental considerations, which incidentally are within the reach of all ordinary mortals. The first was Galega's insight to perceive amidst controversies, the right course to take, and his fortitude to relentlessly pursue this regardless of all odds. His political contribution can be viewed in no better light. The serious threats and cold humiliations he faced when he rose up in support of secession from Nigeria and reunification were situations in which other men would have faltered. Admittedly, the role he played at Lancaster House in London and again at the Fumban constitutional conference was but a remote action in the background of the main events. Yet these roles were vital ones that shaped history. To put it differently, the history of Cameroon should, in all probability, have been different had he acted differently at Lancaster and at Fumban.

Secondly, Galega II struggled in his own modest way throughout life to make this world a better place than he met it (at least his own small corner of it). He was born in a grass-roofed palace.

He died in a modern one that contrasts sharply with the old one in magnificence. The painful etiquette by which people removed their shoes and entered the palace barefoot got discarded in one stroke of reform.

He acceded to the throne when Bali was a typically rural population engaged in subsistence farming. He inspired the people of Bali with a personal example to farm cash crops. His demonstration farm at Gwan introduced new ideas in agriculture, notably oxen farming and the coffee crop, which many farmers in Bali soon turned to.

As a boy he never attended a secondary school[20] and in spite of—or perhaps because of this and utterly regardless of his Catholic upbringing, he travelled as far afield as Calabar to negotiate with Mr. O'Niel, a Protestant Missionary, and other authorities for the opening of the Basel Mission (now, Cameroon Protestant College, Bali. The discussion was successful, and he provided land for the college as he promised during the talks in Calabar.

While in school, he himself went no further than Standard Five in primary school, yet he quietly prepared his successor to climb the education ladder to the highest rung. He thus left the throne to a son with a Doctor of Philosophy (PhD) to meet the challenges of modern times.

Symbolically, Bali grew in his time from a village of subsistence farmers to a flourishing agricultural town capable of feeding itself and exporting food to the neighbouring towns. On the administrative front, Bali grew from a town to a district and to a subdivision, and with these developments came Cameroon government services to Bali.

Galega II will long be remembered by all those who knew him, especially for his forthrightness and shrewdness. He carried

20 And there was no secondary school in Bali when he acceded to the throne.

a radiant personality. He moved with royal dignity and talked with authority. In his heart, he bore deep love for his people and his country. He was and died a true patriot.

3

Economic and Social Setting of the Reign of Galega II (1940–1985)

E.M. Nwana

Prince Vincent Samdala Fonyonga became the 4th Fon of Bali-Nyonga on 30th August 1940 at the age of thirty-four, exactly one year after the 2nd World War had started. In keeping with the Bali-Nyonga tradition of Fons succeeding their grandfathers, the new Fon assumed the new name Galega II and became commonly known as Fon Vincent Samdala Galega II of Bali Nyonga.

Before the new Fon came to the throne, certain social and economic progress had already taken place in Bali Nyonga. Generally speaking, the village had been linked to Bamenda, the capital town and headquarters of the province, by a main road which passed through Bali, Batibo and Widikum to Mamfe, a one-time river port and an economic centre. The Basel Mission had introduced Christianity into the village and built a solid church at Ntanfoang in 1902. A native administration school had existed in the village since 1922. Bali had a main market that was attended by people from far and near every eight days. There was also a nucleus of a daily market at Ntanfoang. There was a handful of houses built out of baked bricks and corrugated iron sheets (zinc). These included the church at Ntanfoang, the Basel Mission pastoral houses at Tikali (Bali) and the main building in the Fon's palace, still uncompleted even till today. All other houses were traditionally built out of bamboo and clay mortar and roofed with dry grass.

A number of Bali people had gone through formal Western education and were making exceptional progress in their respective professions, notably in the Nigerian police force, the Nigerian prison service and in teaching. Pastor Ndifon had been to Germany and back with part of the Bible already translated in Mungaka, the language of the Bali Nyonga people. This language was taught in the vernacular schools and in church doctrine classes in many parts of the North West in order to spread the gospel. Many other Bali people were serving in the Cameroon Development Corporation (CDC) plantations in Fako and Meme Divisions in various capacities. They came home at least once every year during the Lela festival season, bringing along with them many progressive ideas and some material aspects of Western culture.

Another group of Bali Nyonga men found their way to Nigeria through Mamfe and traded with the Ibos of Onitsha, Abakikiki, Enugu, etc. Others went to Calabar in Nigeria along the Cross River. These brought back with them merchandise in the form of gunpowder, soap, cutlasses, sewing machines, cloth, camwood, etc. During their trek to and from Nigeria, they spent some time with villagers along the road and brought back with them some of the foreign cultures that have today become part and parcel of the Bali Nyonga culture. Examples of such foreign cultures are the Nyamkwe dance and Nchibi dance. Names such as Ntianob, Trukang, Okala, etc. were derived from the Ejagham and Bayang villages.

So, in summary, we can say that the new Fon met a certain degree of social and economic advancement already established in Bali.

As we said earlier, the new Fon assumed power during the Second World War. Because of this war, the economic life of most West African regions, including Cameroon, was stifled. Foreign goods became scarce as the attention of the Western powers was now directed only towards the manufacturing of arms and ammunition. Many young men from Bali were recruited as soldiers and sent overseas in support of Britain in the war.

Figure 3.1. Fon V.S. Galega II in his later days.

The scarcity of many Western economic products brought untold hardship to the people, although the situation developed in the people an act of creativity. Bali people produced their own salt (chilum) during this time out of certain leaves or imported locally made salt from Mamfe. They got fire out of steel and flint. Many Bali youth went bare-bodied because of a lack of clothing. The grinding machine was unknown, so foo-foo corn, the staple food of the people was obtained by grinding roasted corn on stone.

There were no streets running through the village as we have now. At best, there were footpaths that were cleared only occasionally by communal labour. There was no pipe-borne water. Various streams and springs were exploited for drinking water. Household utensils included trays made out of spear grass (kukad), calabashes used as containers and as plates, clay pots and clay bowls (kup), wooden mortars, pestles and spoons, stirring sticks for foo-foo corn and sauce, from raffia bamboo.

Other material culture of the people included bamboo beds, chairs, shelves, cupboards, rain covers (mbut and woomti), rectangular baskets (Nkum) for carrying food, etc. People lived a typical village life making their livelihood out of the barest minimum.

The Second World War ended in 1945, and the Western countries with whom we were associated began recovering. The fruit of their economic recovery from this war was manifested in Bali-Nyonga in many forms.

First, a branch of the United African Company (UAC) was established in Bali to buy produce mainly palm kernels and castor oil seeds. Western goods such as cloth, bicycles, soap, cutlasses, salt, gunpowder, etc. were sold in this shop. The presence of this shop, brought in a group of petty contractors who bought palm kernel and castor oil seeds from the hinterland markets and resold these to the UAC for profit. Another group of middlemen retailed some of the merchandise from this shop in the hinterland markets.

During this time, the UAC firm and its sister firm, John Holt, were also established in Mamfe. Mamfe was then linked up to Calabar by the Cross River and launches brought merchandise from the port of Calabar up this river to Mamfe during the rainy season. UAC and John Holt were therefore the main distributors of European goods in Mamfe. In fact, the UAC in Bali was a branch of the Mamfe UAC. The launches that brought Western goods to Mamfe carried back palm kernels, coffee, cocoa, and castor oil seeds.

By 1947, a class of Bali financiers joined the transportation market. They bought lorries or trucks that carried goods from Mamfe to Widikum, Bali and Bamenda. Among these men were the late Ba Gwanulla (Pa 14), the late Augustine Nkwah (Alias Nyam-akundu), the late Pa Simon Forkijah Fogam, and Papa Davidson Mfum Nwana (Alias Trust in God). Other transporters who were not Balis but brought goods to Bali and Bamenda were the late Mr. Aaron, the late Pa Martin Forbin and the late Mr. Eyo. These financiers made Bali a steaming town and a centre for distributing Western goods to the hinterlands.

By 1960, an airstrip was established in Bali, bringing it again into contact with the outside world.

At the time more primary schools were added to the NA school. These included Presbyterian School Tikali, later moved to Njenka, Catholic School Bali town, Catholic School Bawok, Government School Bosah, Government School Gungong, Government School Mbufung, Government School Wosing, etc. Colleges followed in succession. The Cameroon Protestant College, Bali, opened its doors to students in 1949. Self Reliance College opened in 1975, Unity College in 1978, the Rural Artisan Centre (SAR) in 1979, and the Presbyterian handicraft centre in 1967. These schools and colleges produced students for the high schools, advanced professional schools and the universities.

Bali became an administrative district in 1966 and developed into a subdivision in 1979. With the status of a subdivision, many amenities were brought into Bali. Prominent among these are the divisional office, the Gendarmerie post, the police post, the Post Office, the sub treasury, the sub inspectorate of Primary and Nursery education and a host of others. Pipe-borne water, which was introduced in Bali after the 1952 skirmish between the Balis and the Widikums, was expanded and extended to other parts of Bali by SNEC, the National Water Corporation. Electricity was brought into Bali in 1983 by SONEL, the National Electricity Corporation.

The Council clinic that had provided health services to Bali and its environs since the early fifties was (recently) modified to house temporarily a Cottage Hospital. The Catholic health centre at Won is yet another milestone towards the improvement of health in Bali.

The former divisional officer, Mr. Williams, is fondly remembered by most Balis for his drive in the construction of streets and feeder roads within Bali. During his tenure of office, he changed the settlement pattern in Bali from that of compound dwellings to linear settlement. During this period also roads were constructed to link Bosah, Mbufung, Mantum, Mbengwi, Baba I and Pinyin with Bali.

Coffee was introduced in Bali as a cash crop in the late 1950s. Since then, the production of this crop in Bali has raised the status of the Bali Co-operative from a society to a union. The union now produces a little over two hundred tons of coffee annually. Added to this, agricultural posts have been established in some villages in the subdivision to promote modern techniques in farming. Bali subdivision has benefitted from the establishment of a government poultry farm. A few farmers have taken advantage of this and have established their own farms for producing eggs and table birds for sale.

Bali has also witnessed some development in the tourism industry. Safari Lodge was established in 1974, Savannah Hotel in 1966, Hill Top Hotel, now defunct, in 1962 and Tropicana in 1976. The palace witnessed much development. By the end of the 1970s, Bali subdivision as a whole had taken a new look, particularly with regards to house types. Many self-contained bungalows have been built with stone and cement blocks all over the village. The Fon's palace itself had to take a new look and so was rebuilt with stones and concrete and roofed with corrugated iron sheets.

Galega II, himself a Catholic, promoted the establishment of the Catholic Church in Bali to grow alongside its Protestant counterpart. A resident priest was stationed at Bali in 1956. Since then, Bali has made remarkable progress in Catholicism and has produced a Reverend Father. The Catholic missionaries, notably the Reverend Sisters, have rendered tremendous service to the Bali population, especially in the fields of education and health.

During the Fon's reign, Bali was also introduced to the outside world by writers like E.M. Chilver, P.M. Kaberry, M.D.W. Jeffreys and a host of others whom the late Fon personally encouraged.

Until his death in September 1985, all the developments that took place in Bali were attributed to him. He provided the land free of charge for the various development projects, which we have seen above. He used both his political influence and his charisma to lobby for most of the projects and developments which took place in Bali during and even after his reign.

His personal interest in social activities made many young Bali men rally behind him to construct the fence around the palace and the grandstand, which unfortunately was blown off by a whirlwind. He revived the Lela festival and made it a more unifying factor among Bali Nyonga people. Fon. V.S. Galega II will be fondly remembered in Bali for his dynamism in soliciting, initiating and promoting economic and social progress in the subdivision.

The Fon himself personally took the initiative to encourage the formation and organisation of the Bali Nyonga Social, Cultural and Development Association (BASCUDA), in every division in the country. These divisional associations were coordinated at home under the supervision of the Fon by the Bali Nyonga Central Cultural and Development Association (BASCUDA). This central association received money from the divisional associations and used these to carry out approved projects in Bali Nyonga. The permanent fence around the palace and the small hall next to the fence, called *Gwagaa,* used by the scouts during the Lela festive season, were built under the supervision of BASCUDA.

The divisional associations (BASCUDA) were instrumental in collecting money for the Njenka water supply, which later became a government project under SNEC, the state corporation in charge of water. BASCUDAF, the Fako-based divisional association, was instrumental in the levelling of the Lela grounds and in the construction of the grandstand mentioned above. Presently, the Fako and Yaounde branches of BASCUDA are most active and effective in organising their members for the financing of projects at home.

It was as far back as 1947 that Fon V.S. Galega initiated a scholarship scheme for the youth of Bali Nyonga. This scheme was largely financed by the group of young Bali financiers that we mentioned above. Other Bali elites were encouraged to contribute to the financing of this scheme by the Fon. This scheme succeeded in training a number of Bali youth in schools within and outside the country. The scheme only failed when favouritism stepped in and members of the awarding board began to discriminate in the award of scholarships.

Bali Nyonga was not the only village to initiate a scholarship scheme for its youth during this era. Njinikom and the Bayang tribe of Mamfe tried the same scheme with a certain degree of success.

It was only when the then West Cameroon government studied the efforts of these tribes in initiating and contributing to a scholarship fund that the same government introduced the education rating scheme, which provided funds for primary education and made it possible for the government to introduce a four-year free primary education. The four-year free primary education was only abolished in 1976.

Fon. V.S. Galega II had very many progressive ideas and used these ideas in promoting the welfare of his people. In 1965, he discovered that prolonged death celebrations brought untold hardship to bereaved families. He and his traditional council shortened the period for death celebrations to two weeks after the death of a person. The Fon and his council even went further to shorten the period of taboo on widows. He also reduced some of the mourning practices, such as the wearing of black attire. These reforms have benefitted the people economically. They now have time after the death celebration to carry out such economic activities as farming, trading and catering for the education of their children. During his address to the people during the Lela festival, he many times emphasised on the maximum utilisation of land for economic purposes such as food and cash crop farming, the construction of modern houses, the construction of fish ponds and the planting of economic trees, e.g., the eucalyptus and fruit trees. The Fon totally wiped out of Bali main town straying animals which were a menace to the population.

One of the important social reforms for which the Fon will forever be remembered is the injection of a class of highly literate elites into the various traditional organs of his government, notably the institutions of Nkom and Sama.

Galega II was the first Fon to clothe his wives in the North-West Province and went around to encourage his colleagues to do the same. It is said that Galega II, a close friend to the Fon of Bafut, Achirimbi II, forced the latter's wives to be clothed by providing the first dresses to them. While Fon V.S. Galega II's father's wives went topless and distinguished themselves from other wives in the tribe by wearing a string of cowries around their skulls, Galega II's wives covered their heads with clothes after the fashion of Muslim wives.

In fact, nudity disappeared in Bali Nyonga in 1949 through the efforts of Fon. V.S. Galega II who decreed that no person should go nude in Bali-Nyonga after that year.

The essence of any human association has always been to cater to the welfare of its members. In the early years of Fon Galega II's reign, traditional associations dealt with common problems of the community, namely the maintenance of law and order, the performance of communal labour, the settling of disputes, and the promotion of a harmonious life in society.

When British indirect rule disappeared with the British colonial masters and a more centralised authority emerged with independence, most of the traditional associations had to modify their structures and functions to meet the needs of the new society. They now function to encourage, preserve and promote the Bali Nyonga culture. They have led to the revival of many traditional values and have now reinforced the respect for elders. They also operate savings accounts and encourage thrift and loans. With special savings, these associations are able to celebrate births, marriages, and deaths and to come to the aid of any member who is desperately in need of financial assistance.

Figure 3.2. The burial: The effigy of Galega II is borne to its resting place by kingmakers.

Side by side with the traditional association, new associations have grown whose membership is drawn from the educated elites. Some of these associations include **Kadnvi** in Bamenda, **Kadndap** in Yaounde and Buea, the Catholic Women's Association (CWA), the Christian Women's Fellowship (CWF), etc. These provide the platform for members to express their ideas and pursue common ideals. They have formal rules of debate and written constitutions.

They take minutes and record them. They have secretaries and treasurers, and they keep accurate financial records that may be audited as needed. These offices are usually well defined in written constitutions and differ from the old traditional associations in that the traditional associations operated without written constitutions. Officers are elected. Although these modern associations perform the same economic roles as the traditional associations, they operate on a more sophisticated scale.

Fon V.S. Galega II himself encouraged these modern associations whose membership are open to all Cameroonians of good will, by visiting them and encouraging his wives and children to participate in some of them.

In summary, the late Fon Vincent Samdala Galega II lived through change, solicited change, initiated, encouraged, and promoted change, especially in the fields of social and economic reforms.

4

The Traditional Political Institution of Bali Nyonga

An Outline of their Roles in the Installation of a New Fon of Bali

V.P.K. Titanji

GENERAL INTRODUCTION

Bali Nyonga is one of the traditional communities in the North West Province of Cameroon. In spite of the rapid winds of modernisation that are changing both the face and customs of our traditional communities, the Balis have repeatedly manifested their cultural identity in their regular annual festivals of Lela and Voma dances, which have become popular, attracting onlookers from all over the Republic and some foreign countries.

The custodians of traditional cultural activities in the North West Province are the traditional monarchs, the Fons. As government-appointed administrators are gradually but firmly replacing them, the Fons have turned to emphasising their roles as custodians of culture and traditions of the people. It is within this context that this paper examines the institutions that confer, both moral and administrative authority on a newly appointed Fon among the Bali Nyonga of the North West of Cameroon.

On September 18, 1985, His Royal Highness Galega II, Fon of Bali from 1940-1985, died. About two weeks later, his son, Dr. Dohsang, was enthroned as Fon of Bali. According to tradition, he took a name derived from that of his grandfather and is called Ganyonga III. The death of H.R.H. Galega II ushered in a season of mourning accompanied by intense cultural and political activities within Bali Nyonga—activities which had repercussions in other neighbouring chiefdoms as they joined Bali Nyonga in mourning. In the midst of these activities, there were consultations about the rules and procedures as well as traditions associated with the inauguration of a new Fon. Apart from a brief mention of this in the report by Kaberry and Chilver (1961), no documents have appeared on the subject of the installation of a Fon among the Balis. The purpose of this article is to describe the role of traditional institutions in installing and legitimising the Fon and to show how these institutions functioned in 1985.

Although the traditional institutions of Bali Nyonga have been described previously, their role in the installation of the Fon has received very little attention. Herein, we shall describe these institutions, including some aspects which were often omitted in previous studies. We shall also present the dynamic interaction of various groups and briefly describe their evolution during the reigns of each of the three principal Fons of Bali, namely, Galega I, Fonyonga II and Galega II whose reigns stretched from the last quarter of the last century to 1985. For ease of presentation, we have divided this article into three parts: Part I deals with the structure of the various branches of the traditional system, Part II with the installation of a new Fon, and Part III describes the executive branch.

PART ONE

THE TRADITIONAL INSTITUTIONS OF BALI NYONGA

Bali Nyonga is traditionally a monarchical state, headed by the Fon. In precolonial times, the Fon was vested with vast powers within his fondom and could arbitrate on all matters, including those concerning life and death. He was the military leader, a representative of the people before the gods of the land, but not a divine king. Far from exercising power single-handedly, the Fon shared authority with some traditional institutions which he nominally headed. Under certain circumstances he delegated some of his powers to those institutions. It was very important that these institutions support the Fon in his decisions since membership of the institutions usually comprised influential members of the community, whose collaboration was needed for the exercise of royal authority.

Traditional institutions in Bali Nyonga can be divided into two groups, namely, political and religious institutions. Political institutions are represented by the *Kom, Tsinted* and *Fonte* while the religious institutions are the *Voma* and *Lela* cults.

Religious institutions had the duty to install and initiate the new Fon into the mysteries of kingship, while political institutions provided him with the support and legitimacy to govern. Today these institutions have evolved considerably and all combine to form what has come to be known as the Bali Traditional Council. At the same time, the distinction between political and religious institutions is no longer very sharp, since individuals may belong to both groups at the same time. Besides, both the religious and political institutions are now involved in the administration of the traditional society.

THE RELIGIOUS INSTITUTIONS

The two most important traditional institutions concerned with chieftaincy rites are the *Voma* from which king-makers are drawn, and the *Lela* which is involved in swearing in the newly installed *Fon* and initiating him in the secrets of the land. Although both the *Voma* and the *Lela* drew their inspirations principally from religious cults, as will be seen later, they also performed political and military functions. Our immediate concern is to examine the history, structure and functions of each of the religious institutions.

Voma

The *Voma* cult exists in all the *Chamba* fondoms of the North West Province. It was originally a non-royal institution concerned with fertility rites. It was the responsibility of *Voma,* in its yearly celebrations, to invoke the gods of the land to make man, his animals and land fertile. The religious functions of *Voma* also included fighting evil spirits which were believed to plague the land in times of difficulty. Apart from these purely spiritual functions, the *Voma* contained among its members great traditional healers, who took care of the sick, usually for only a token fee of firewood or a fowl. Some of the ailments still treated by the *Voma* society today include various eye infections, toothache, diarrhoea and female infertility.

Very early in Bali's history, before the battle of Bafu-Fondong, which led to the death of Gawolbe and the division of the Bali ethnic group into 7 different fondoms, the *Voma* society also discharged the duties of a regulatory fraternity. The *Voma* contained at the time a regulatory fraternity known as *Vomdzaana* which had the power to institute injunctions on disputed property, banish criminals and execute murderers. Later, just before the German colonisation of Cameroon, the prerogatives of the *Vomdzaana* society were usurped by the *Ngumba,* which is the equivalent of the well-established *Kwifon* group known to operate among the Tikars of the North West Province. It should be pointed out that the *Ngumba* does not wield as much power among the Balis as the *Kwifon* does among the Tikars. For example, unlike the *Kwifon,* the *Ngumba* is not concerned with chieftaincy rites; it only acts as a police organisation in keeping the peace and executing the decisions of the Fons.

Origins of the Voma Institution

Voma is an ancient fertility cult of non-royal descendants of the Bali Chamba. Its leaders were originally guards of the Fon, hence the title of *Nwana,* which means "guard" was given to these leaders. Subsequently, the Nwana became king-makers, a role which enhanced their political participation in the affairs of the fondom. Although *Voma's* development has been uninterrupted in other Bali fondoms, its recent evolution in Bali Nyonga began during the reign of Galega I in the 1860s. Since *Voma is* a male cult, it could not be maintained in Bali Nyonga during the reign of *Na'Nyonga,* who was the female founder—monarch of the group. Tradition has it that Na'Nyonga and her followers separated from the other Bali groups during the struggles which followed the succession of Gawolbe. Subsequently, the royal power of the group fell upon her son Nyongpasi (Fonyonga I). Nyongpasi was succeeded by Galega I, the first Bali Nyonga monarch to settle at the present site. In his bid to reconstruct in Bali Nyonga the original Chamba system, he decided to reintroduce *Voma* into Bali Nyonga from Bali Gham, which, unlike the other Bali fondoms, had maintained close links with Bali Nyonga.

The person who actually brought *Voma* objects of divination and taught the Bali Nyonga people the secrets of the cult was known as *Ngo.* He was rewarded by Galega I, who gave him one of his daughters as a wife. Ngo's son from his princess wife later succeeded him and was given the royal title of Tita Ngo in respect of his royal connection.

Oral tradition is vague about the factors that affected the distribution of leadership positions when *Voma* was re-established in Bali Nyonga. However, it seems that Galega I was careful to organise the cult in such a manner as to maintain full control over it. Although *Voma* was meant to be an institution for non-royals, Galega I nevertheless introduced members of his family into the cult, to keep a check on the commoners to whom Voma belonged. Furthermore, important duties were distributed among several leaders to avoid the emergence of a single powerful member who could challenge royal authority.

In the actual distribution of functions, Galega I appointed *Gwanvoma* as the administrative head of the *Voma,* in charge of public celebrations and day-to-day running of the society. Tita Langa who was maternally related to Galega I and belonged to the powerful Vomdzaana organisation was appointed to head certain important rites administered by the *Voma* society.

Our informants inferred that the *Vomdzaana* group was present and performed its police functions all along within the context of the Lela Society, whose evolution in Bali Nyonga was never interrupted by the reign of a female monarch. Nwanyedla (Doh Nwana) was to be the custodian of all the cult objects of the *Voma* society. Yabala Njingwadnyam (Tita Nji I), who was the first son of Galega I, was appointed to be *Nwan-Vaksi,* the representative of blood royals in the *Voma* institution. Tita Nyagang, Tita Musing and Tita Ngo were also made leaders. The position of *Lamgwa's,* the officer in charge of smith works went to Nji, a descendant of the Ti-Gawolbe ethnic group that produced many craftsmen. Naturally, the Fon was the overall head of the Voma.

Following reforms carried out in the Voma institution during the reign of Galega II, Fogam (alias Fokejah), Tambombo Fufunjuh (alias Caspa), Tita Labi were elevated to the rank of *Nwana.* Our informants stated that Fogam and Tambombo Fufunjuh were incorporated into the leadership group because of their expertise in dental care, gained during military service in the German colonial army. Tita Labi, who was related to Galega I through his mother, was raised to the leadership position because of his long-term association with the palace and the distinguished service he performed in the field of cultural animation. *Naka is* also known to be among the *Nwana* though he has not often asserted himself. The appointments to the office of *Nwana* were hereditary and most of the successors of the original appointees still live in Bali Nyonga today; they have continued to perform the functions attributed to their predecessors in the Voma society.

Structure and Function of the Voma Institution

The Voma is organised hierarchically into four grades beginning from the top with Ba-Nwana, followed in order of decreasing importance by Ba Tikwang'a, Bon-Voma and Vom-Keina.

Ba-Nwana (Nwan-Billa)

At the present, there are thirteen positions of Nwana, of which nine are the original Nwana. The Nwana are king-makers. They are responsible for the burial, installation and initiation of the Fon into the secrets of Bali society and educating him in the art of government. Tita Langa is the person who actually anoints the Fon and performs all the rites that are necessary to confirm the successor as Fon. This role falls on Tita Langa because his predecessor was the descendant of Gangsin, the father of Gawolbe II, the monarch who led out the Balis from the original homeland. In Bali tradition it is ego's sister's sons collectively referred to as *Bundzad* or *Lekasiwaa*, who install him to hereditary positions when deaths occur in large families.

Each Nwana is specially ordained upon appointment during a special secret ceremony known as *Ma we musun or Ma pob musun.* This particular ordination ceremony is part of the Bali chieftainship rite and is followed by all men appointed by the Fon to perform special functions in the palace. For ease of understanding, we shall simply refer to it as *initiation into the Bali state cult.*

Tikwanga Voma

These are senior members of the *Voma* society who are not *Nwana.* They are recruited from the group of ordinary *Voma* members (Bon Voma) on merit. The Tikwanga may substitute a *Nwana* during certain ceremonies, but not in the installation of the *Fon.* The title of Tikwanga is also given to ward heads who administratively belong to the group of *Kom Ngong,* but do not have the protocol rank of nkom.

Bon Voma

Literally, this means *children of Voma*. This is a group of junior members of the *Voma* society. Some of them are allowed to join the *Voma* because of their ability to perform *Voma* music. Others are nominated by different members of the *Nwana* group to act as valets for them during the meetings of the *Voma* society. Both the *Bon Voma* and *Tikwanga* undergo an initiation ceremony called *Ma Lab Voma* or *Ma Lab Dola* before they are allowed full membership of the *Voma*.

Vom-Keina

Literally this word means, *wives of Voma*. Although *Voma* is predominantly a male cult, women may be associated with it as external choristers to sing *Voma* music during the public appearances of the society. Every Nwana and Tikwanga is expected to nominate one or several female members of his family to join the Vom-Keina. The appointee may be his wife or daughter or some other close relative. The Vom-Keina do not have the right to participate in the secret meetings of the *Voma*.

The Voma Shrine (Dola)

The Voma society holds its meetings in a shrine called Dola. The Dola is a building in a secluded area. Around the Dola are planted many of the Voma medicinal herbs. A more detailed description of the shrine and its contents is forbidden by tradition. In Bali Nyonga, there are three Dolas. These are Dola Ngu, or (Great Shrine), found at Ntaiton Quarter, Dola Tsenye, found at Tsenye's compound at Tikali Quarter and Dola Tandzong, now found at Tita Nji's compound.

The Dola Ngu is the meeting place of the Voma Society. It is here that the Nwanas meet to make sacrifices and take decisions affecting the Voma festivals. The Dola Ngu also houses the "planting" of Voma in October (Vomsoa) to mark the beginning of the planting season for millet. The other two Dolas, i.e. Dola Tsenye and Dola Tandzong, house the "first fruits" of Voma and are called Vom-Langu.

Cultural Activities of the Voma Institution

We have already stated that the leaders of the *Voma* (Ba Nwana) are charged with the important task of installing the Fon in Bali. Apart from this and other duties described above, the Voma institution is very active all year round. It stages major annual rites in January or February at the end of the dry season, presumably to invoke the return of the rains and again in October to mark the beginning of the planting season. It animates burials and funerals of important members of the Bali community, including those of its members when they occur.

Unlike the *Lela* festival, which is discussed below, the Voma festival is less well-known outside Bali. This is perhaps because *Voma* is a cult for men, almost to the exclusion of women, whereas *Lela* is a popular festival. Besides, there are many taboos associated with the activities of Voma and its reputation for mystical and occult practices makes it more dreaded and less popular. This notwithstanding, anyone living or visiting Bali Nyonga from October through March is bound to encounter one or several of the public manifestations of Voma.

Early in October, the Voma ritual begins with a nocturnal ceremony conducted by the Nwana at the *Dola Ngu*. The sound of Voma music (at night) informs the villagers of the beginning of Voma celebrations. During the week, corn beer is brewed and food and other drinks are procured for the celebrations.

On an appointed afternoon, usually the third day after the market day (known as Ndansi in Mungaka), the Voma society makes an exit from *Dola Ngu* to bless the village and at the same time initiate public celebrations of the big Voma dance. Led by Gwanvoma, the Voma orchestra tunes Voma music and makes a tour of the village following a well-defined itinerary. During this processional tour, both the Nwana and the orchestra are followed by large crowds of non-members, including men and boys. The *Vom-Keina* trail behind, taking care not to see the Voma. The procession stops at the compound of each deserving noble, where it is given corn beer and corn cakes *(Suga).* At each compound, Gwanvoma pours libations at the gate and invokes the gods to bless the families and all present therein to be fertile and bring forth many more children.

At the end of the first day of exit, Voma encamps at the compound of Ndzingum, one of the Nwanas who descended from the family of blacksmiths. Smith works are associated with numerous taboos and rites and it is noteworthy that the Voma stays at the compound of a blacksmith during its first night out of the shrine.

The second day is known as the day of ascent, when Voma dance is staged at the Fon's palace. The procession from Ndzingum's compound in Ntanfoang Quarter to the dancing piazza in the palace is again led by the Nwana. Voma is then received by the Fon, who on this occasion is surrounded by nobles known as Nwana Fon (or the Fon's Voma Leaders), to distinguish them from the hereditary leaders of the Voma society described above. After the ceremonial blessing of the palace, serious playing and dancing of Voma music begins. The Voma dance lasts for three days and three nights. During this period, the Voma orchestra is quartered in a special rest house in the palace called Gwa'ga. Junior members of the society, under the supervision of some Nwana, are in charge of guarding the orchestra during this period.

The Voma dances are usually staged between 4 and 6 pm every day. During this period, no other type of music is allowed in the village. Members of the Voma give sumptuous parties in their compounds to which friends and relatives are invited.

On the fourth day, the Voma rounds up the occasion by blessing more compounds and the village. It then returns to the Dola Ngu or the Great Shrine.

The festival of the "First fruits" Voma is a one-day event in January to February. Malcolm Green has described the atmosphere of this day very vividly (Green, 1984). The main objective of the event is to bless both the first millet and the seeds for the next season's planting. During the whole day, the entire village remains indoors and only members of the Voma move about the streets performing the blessing. On this day, the Voma-Langu, which is believed to possess very potent mystical powers, comes out to neutralise evil spirits and bad medicines which people may have brought into the land.

One relatively less known manifestation of the Voma society is the formal closing of the Voma year known as Vomnung'a. On this day, the Nwana gather at the Dola Ngu to close the Voma year. The ceremony is not open to the public, but we were told that on this day, rites are conducted to "reduce" some of the mystical powers of the Voma objects so that they can be handed over for safekeeping by Doh Nwana until the following year. At this occasion, the Fon usually gives the Nwana a ram, which is slaughtered and used in the sacrifices forming part of the Vomnung'a ceremony.

Initiation of the Fon and Nobles into the Bali State Cult

The rites of initiation into senior traditional associations in Bali Nyonga are kept secret from non-members. In our investigations, we were told that the ceremony cryptically known as *catching the turaco bird,* literally translated as *Ma we musung or Ma pob Musung,* is the most important rite that a Bali man can undergo. Only the Fon, the Nwana, some members of the Lela and other individuals selected by the Fon may be initiated in this way. We learnt that only those who observe strict sexual morality, that is, non-adulterers, may be initiated. Once initiated, they enter a brotherhood of confidence with the Fon and other initiates. The initiation ceremony is performed jointly by the Voma and Lela societies, the former being represented by Gwanvoma and the latter by Tita Langa. The site of the initiation ceremony is the Wolela (Lela Shrine) located on the dancing piazza in front of the Fon's palace. The ceremony takes place in the early hours of the morning in utter secrecy in the presence of the Fon. When a new Fon is installed, he too must undergo this initiation rite. The exact manner of conducting the rite at the Wolela is a well-guarded secret of the Voma and Lela societies.

Following the rites conducted at the Wolela, the initiated person, accompanied by Gwanvoma and one or two Nwana, return to his compound to complete a semi-public phase of the rite. For three days and three nights, the initiate is secluded in his house, where he lies on plantain leaves on the floor, probably as a test of endurance. He is not allowed to talk with ordinary non-initiated people. He is guarded by Gwanvoma or any other Nwana, designated for the purpose to avoid his violating ritual taboos. During these days, the initiated person is instructed by the Nwana on the secrets of the land. He begins each day by undergoing daily purification rites at a stream, where he undergoes ritual bathing. At the end of the three days, the initiated person is presented to the public, in a ceremony during which the Nwana decides whether the initiation has been successful or not.

In the account which follows, we describe the presentation ceremony of an initiated person as observed by us in mid-1956. (From the recent accounts of our informants, this procedure has remained essentially the same). On the day of presentation, a small stone altar was raised in a clearing near the initiate's house. Close to this altar was planted a trimmed forked branch of a fig tree. When the invitees, the Nwana and relatives of the initiate had gathered at the clearing (*Ntan-Musing*) the initiate was led by the Nwana to the clearing. He was holding a spear *(Dingsoga)* in his right hand and dressed in a white battle dress *(Palewa).*

Upon arrival at the clearing, the Nwana formed a semi-circle around the altar with the given initiate standing in front of the altar. Then Gwanvoma was given a cock by the first wife of the initiate. After feeding the cock with a few drops of corn beer, Gwanvoma sacrificed it by decapitating it with a sacrificial knife (Saawa). The decapitated cock mounted a vigorous death struggle, which was closely watched by the Nwana in order to determine if the initiation was successful. We were told that, depending upon the manner in which the cock struggled after decapitation, they could tell if the initiation had been successful or not. On this particular occasion, Gwanvoma declared the initiation successful. The royal drum, Dangdang, was played to mark the beginning of jubilation and feasting. Thereafter, the initiated person was allowed to enjoy such prerogatives as decorating his cap with a red feather, eating Lela and Voma medicine cooked in a special pot (Mbang Musing) and entering the private quarters of the Fon.

THE LELA INSTITUTION

The Lela institution and the ceremonies surrounding it have been discussed in great detail by previous investigators (Soh, 1978; Ndangam and Nwana, 1981). Here we will concentrate only on those ceremonies that concern the royal institution. Unlike Lela, the Voma society, which was dominated by non-royals, the Lela was a royal institution, led mainly by descendants of the royal family. Its ceremonies embody rites associated with chieftainship and warfare.

Considering its religious role, the Lela society is in charge of the Wolela (Lela Shrine), where sacrifices are made at least twice yearly to appease the gods. After the inauguration of the Fon, he is led in a public ceremony to "mount" the Wolela which is located on the dance piazza in front of the Palace. This symbolic gesture indicates Lela's acceptance of the Fon as a leader of the Bali people and a mediator between the people and their gods.

Like the Voma, the Lela institution is hierarchically organised with the Fon at the head. The Fon may delegate certain of his powers to various members of the group. The various groups of authority in the *Lela* society, beginning from the highest to the lowest, are the *Sama,* the *Tutuwan* and the *Gwe*. To these may be added a miscellaneous group of guards. Membership of the *Lela* society can only be gained through nomination by the *Fon* and by inheritance. Positions in the Sama group are either hereditary or non-hereditary. The *Sama* who perform special duties at various ceremonies of the *Lela* society usually occupy hereditary positions. Those co-opted into the *Sama* because of their knowledge of *Lela* music hold non-hereditary titles, which, however, could be inherited by their successors at the discretion of the *Fon.* In 1985, the following were identified as hereditary title holders in the *Sama* society:

- Tita Langa
- Tita Nji
- Tita Fonkwa
- Tita Yebid
- Tita Sua
- Tita Bamoh
- Banyuga Gwanlima
- Naaka
- Tita Nukuna
- Tita Nyagasa
- Tita Doh Kundzuma
- Fogakoh

The non-hereditary title holders of the Sama today include, among others, Gwandi, Gwendzeng, Foyan, Trukang and Saila

Fohtung. Altogether, there are nearly 30 members in the Sama group. Recently, H.R.H. Ganyonga III named two of his prince brothers, Tita Duga and Tita Sama, to this prestigious group.

Tutuwan

Tutuwan (also known as Tutunwan) are Flag-bearers in the traditional army. They are appointed by the Fon on personal merit. Ordinarily, their positions are non-hereditary except when the Fon decides otherwise. Flag-bearers automatically lose their positions upon the death of the Fon and may be replaced by new appointees. The head of the Tutuwan group is Tita Nyagang. He also heads the Gwe, who are described more fully below. The leader's position is also non-hereditary, and a new Tita Nyagang may be named on the advent of a new Fon. In practice, the Fons have tended, during the last two generations, to maintain the titles of Tutuwan within the same families. The number of *Tutuwans* varies between 2 and 3, plus 4 substitutes, making a total of 6-7. They can be identified in any Lela festival near the two traditional emblems of the Balis. They usually wear a uniform and stand very close to the traditional flags. Each of the *Tutuwans* or their substitutes is ritually initiated into the Bali state cult and is treated with great respect in the community. Tita Nyagang Mundoni represents the Fon at public sacrifices at the Lela stream during the annual dance. He can be easily identified carrying the insignia, which comprises two spears called *Dingwasa* and a third spear called *Dingsoga* (Nwana, 1985). It is important to point out that the *Tutuwan* are not descendants of the royal family.

Gwe and the Guards

Chilver (1961) described the Gwe as spies who, in public ceremonies, acted as fools or jesters. This description is still essentially true. Because the Lela society is the custodian of war medicine, it is only natural that the traditional spying and security organisation be associated with it. In precolonial times, the Gwe acted as informants and spies for the Fon. Today, they play the role of scouts in public functions, particularly Lela festivals. Each Gwe is personally selected by the Fon. His position may be inherited by one of his sons. Some of the famous Gwe still living today are Gwe Nchanyam, Gwe Pamuga, Gwe Tateh, Gwe Vadla and Gwe Mumbamti. As a rule, the Gwe are not descendants of the royal family. It must be emphasised that because of their non-royal origin, the Gwe and Tutuwan do not take part in officiating at the sacrifices offered at the Wolela. This is the prerogative of the hereditary members of the Sama group. During the reign of Fonyonga II, there were no less than 60 known Gwe; today, there are hardly over a dozen, a finding which reflects the reduced number of military activities in Bali Nyonga.

The Fon may appoint certain individuals he trusts as special armed guards to reinforce the Gwe. These individuals do not, however, indulge in jesting at public ceremonies.

THE ROLE OF THE LELA INSTITUTION IN THE RITUAL INSTALLATION OF THE FON

The role of Lela in the installation of the Fon is next in importance to that of the Voma society. They play three important parts in the initiation process. First, the initiation rite into the state cult is done at the Lela shrine in the presence of the representative of both the Voma and Lela societies. Secondly, two senior members of the Lela are also leading members of the Voma. These are Tita Langa, the principal king-maker, and Tita Nji, who is the representative of the royal descendants in the Voma institution. During the public presentation of the Fon after his inauguration, the Fon is led by the king-makers in a public ceremony with full pomp and pageantry to ceremonially mount the shrine. This is one of the most important manifestations of the intimate collaboration which exists between the Voma and Lela societies in maintaining the royal institution. Finally, prominent members of the Lela played key roles in ensuring that the wills of the deceased monarchs were respected and that, in each case, the correct heir was installed as Fon. This more or less describes the supportive role of the Lela society in the installation of the Fon.

Figure 4.1. Ganyonga III leading a procession during the Lela Festival.

Tsinted

The *Tsinted* are a miscellaneous group of courtiers, military leaders, lobbyists, diplomats and servants engaged in the daily administration in the Fon's palace. Members of the Tsinted are recruited from among twins and families that were traditionally associated with the group. There are no special initiation rites for the members, but the Fon may decide to have some of them initiated into the Lela or Voma societies. There are two ranks within the Tsinted group, namely *Kom Tsinted* and *Bon Tsinted.*

Kom Tsinted

There are four Kom Tsinted, all of them hereditary titleholders. All of the Kom Tsinted have risen to the rank of military commander or Tita. Each Nkom Ntsinted (singular) plays a special function in the palace. The pinnacle of the power of Kom Tsinted came during the reign of Fonyonga II, when each of them was appointed as a patron (Tadmanji = father of the road) entrusted with the administration of one or more colonised villages comprising what has been called the Bali empire (Soh, 1985). Today, the following hereditary positions of Kom Tsinted exist in Bali Nyonga:

- Tita Foncham
- Tita Fokum
- Tita Mufut
- Tita Fofam

Together with Tita Sikod (see below), the Kom Tsinted were in charge of distributing gunpowder, food and doing other administrative duties in the palace.

Bon Tsinted

These are mainly valets and men-servants in the palace. Many of them are twins; some are given to serve in the palace by their families, and others are directly selected by the Fon. In the course of their duties, they may become very important and may acquire a title for themselves, for example, among the Kom Ngong when such vacancies do occur.

The Kom

The rank of Kom has been reported to be a creation of Nyongpasi (Chilver, 1961). However, it is probable that this institution is older since it also exists in other Bali fondoms. The Kom are the Bali Nyonga equivalent of modern ministers of government appointed by the Fon from the population on personal merit. A Nkom (singular) must be a man who has shown leadership qualities, is prosperous, fair-minded, intelligent and has an imposing physical appearance. He must have distinguished himself in the public service of the village and must be personally wealthy. In bygone days, a Nkom was also a distinguished warrior and a man of valour.

In the administrative set-up of Bali, the Kom wield enormous authority and are directly answerable to the Fon. They may settle cases in their quarters, or sit as judges in the traditional court, which holds on the palace piazza. As a group, the Kom assist the Fon in decision-making by supplying him with information and advice. They may be called upon to represent the Fon in public ceremonies and are in charge of transmitting royal proclamations to the public. Like other traditional institutions, the Kom fall into two important groups, namely *Kom Ba'ni* and *Kom Ngong*.

Kom Ba'ni

These are hereditary titleholders whose predecessors were Kom as far back as the days of Nyongpasi (Fonyonga I). They are also referred to as Kom Ba'ni (Kaberry and Chilver, 1961) or Kom Kwatad (Soh, 1978). The following were identified as Kom Ba'ni, given in order of protocol importance:

1. Tita Kuna
2. Tita Kunkah (Gwanchelleng)
3. Tita Gwandiku
4. Gwansenyam (vacant)
5. Gwananji
6. Gwaabe
7. Gwandi

The use of the title of Tita by three of the Kom Ba'ni emphasises the leadership position of these individuals; it does not designate royal descent as is often the case with princes.

Figure 4.2. A group of dignitaries among the Komfon in Bali Nyonga during the funeral of HRH Galega II.

Kom Ngong or Kom

These are titleholders appointed by personal merit to assist the Fon in the running of public affairs. Historically, the office of *Kom Ngong* seems to date back to Fonyonga II, since both Nyongpasi and Galega I maintained the Kom kwatad listed above in their war councils. The titles of Kom Ngong may or may not be inherited by their descendants, depending upon the qualities of the successor. In practice, their titles have tended to be inheritable. During the reign of Galega II the Kom Ngong and Kom Kwatad organised themselves into a society of their own known as Ndakum Bakom. The objective of their society was to encourage solidarity in the public service of the Bali fondom. Upon ascent to the throne, H.R.H. Ganyonga III inherited 47 titleholders of this group distributed as follows: 7 Kom Mfon or Kom Kwatad, 17 Kom Fonyonga appointed by Fonyonga

II, and 27 Kom Galega appointed by Galega II. Ganyonga II has appointed 6 Kom so far making a total of 57 titleholders in this important group.

To the group of Kom may be added Tikwanga or titular ward-heads who also acted as military advisers to the Fon. This title is also used to designate some senior members of the Voma (see above). The original hereditary Tikwanga were Tita Sikod (of Mbangom), Tita Kung (of Buti) Tita Juwan, Kunjamvalla, and Ntondab. In public ceremonies the Tikwanga sit with the Kom and enjoy the honorific address of *Ndey*.

Fonte' (Sub-Chiefs)

Sub-chiefs emerged in Bali Nyonga as a result of the incorporation of non-Yani groups into the original Yani elements that came from the Chamba homeland in the last century. As the Balis migrated southwards, waging wars of conquest, they formed military alliances with certain groups which eventually became part and parcel of Bali, joining them in their raids down to their present settlement. These groups were nominally headed by sub-chiefs who paid tribute to the Fon of Bali. Many of them retained their titles of chief (Fo) and their original languages, which are now spoken mostly during religious rites. There are two groups of sub-chiefs, namely, Fonte' Ba'ni and Fonte' Banten.

Fonte' Ba'ni

These are sub-chiefs whose people were associated with the Bali before the battle of Bafu-Fondong. They are five Fonte' Ba'ni namely: Fombonjong (Fumujeng), Fo-Kemban (both Buti), Fo-Ti-kali (Tikali) and Fo-Ti (Ti-Gawolbe).

Fonte' Banten (or Lolo)

There are nine Fonte' Banten: FoKundem, Fo-Ngiam, Fo-Sangam, Fo-Won, Fo-Ngod, Fo-Sang, Fo-Fuleng, Fo-Set and

Fomunyam. To these may be added the following sub-chiefs who fall within the functional definition of Fonte' Banten (as those who came under the influence of Bali Nyonga after the Battle of Bafu-Fondong: Fombelu, Fobossah, Fowock and Fombufung. But these are not of Lolo stock. It is worthwhile noting that these last four do not participate in ritual ceremonies in which they are represented by Fokunyang.

Fogako' represents the Peli or Bali Kontan, who were the first to occupy the present site before they were defeated by Bali Nyonga under the leadership of Galega I. But he is considered a *Fonte' Ba'ni* because of his *Chamba* origin. Some people claim today that the two *Lela* emblems represent both *Peli* and *Yani* populations. It is known for certain, however, that the second flag was copied by Zintgraff and presented to Galega I as a gift. It may be that upon consecrating the flag, Galega I, a keen tactician, found it politically expedient to proclaim that the second or female flag represented the *Peli* whose flag had earlier been suppressed by him. As a member of the Lela society, *Fogako'* belongs to one of the pillars of the royal institution in Bali.

The role of the Fonte' in installing the Fon is limited to supplying him with mystical powers which he is believed to need for the discharge of his royal functions. In this respect, Bangu who represents the Kang Group and the powerful Bati elements in Bali plays an important role in blessing the palace during the funeral and installation ceremonies. Like the Kom, the Fonte' help the Fon in the administration of their respective quarters. In days gone by, the Fonte' and Kom-Kwatad formed the war council that advised the Fon on military matters.

The Ngumba

Historically, the Ngumba society is a very young organisation in Bali Nyonga. It has its roots in the defunct Vomdzaana and the suppressed Kwifon societies of the Banten allies. The Ngumba inherited the peacekeeping and judiciary functions of Vomdzaana but did not inherit the king-making function of the latter or of the Kwifon. The king-making function remained a prerogative of the Voma society.

The Ngumba draws its members mainly from among the sons of the Fon's sisters, half-sisters and nieces, collectively known as Lekasiwaa or Bundzad. Princes, the children of the Fon's brothers, half-brothers or male cousins and all females are forbidden to become members of this society. Some Tsinted and Kom Ngong also hold positions among the Ngumba. Membership in Ngumba is formalised by the Fon's nomination. Positions are inheritable. The titular head of the Ngumba is called Tandangu (father of the house of Ngumba).

The Ngumba holds its meetings in its own palace, called Nted Ngumba. It is built close to the Fon's palace to enable it to communicate directly with the Fon. In public ceremonies and at funerals of important nobles, vanguards of the Ngumba may be seen wearing feather tunics and carrying clubs and spears as a symbol of great power. The Ngumba is responsible for maintaining order during public ceremonies, instituting injunctions and enforcing decisions taken by the Fon. Because of its high-powered membership, the Ngumba is an essential arm of the royal institution.

PART TWO

THE INSTALLATION OF THE FON OF BALI

Choice of the Successor

Bali Nyonga is a patrilineal society where a son inherits the property and title of his father. Traditionally, the crown prince is the first son to be born on the throne. This rule, however, is not inviolable because the Fon may choose another deserving son as his successor. For this reason, the identity of the heir remains a closely guarded secret known only to the Fon and a few of his closest associates, usually members of the Nwana group, who are sworn to keep the secret and to divulge it only after the death of the Fon.

From the above description, it is clear that the Fon alone chooses his successor among his sons. What happens to the Fon who leaves no son to inherit him? What happens in the case of a sudden death where no will has been made? Although no such occasion is known to have arisen, our informants felt that in such a case only the royal family could choose the successor among the deceased Fon's brothers and half-brothers or from among the sons he might have had before he was installed. This point is very important because it emphasises a basic difference between the Bali culture and that of neighbouring fondoms. Although there are king makers in Bali, it is not their prerogative to choose the successor of the Fon if such a choice had not been made by the deceased Fon himself. One should point out that the term "royal family" is used here to mean the extended royal family, comprising the immediate sons and daughters of the deceased Fon, his brothers and half-brothers, as well as his uncles and cousins or their successors. Curiously enough, the wives of the Fon would not be allowed to participate in the choice of the Fon's successor.

Among the Tikars, for example, the Kwifon would intervene in such matters. In Bali Nyonga the Ngumba as well as the Voma societies are nominally non-royal institutions which do not decide on succession in the royal household. This notwithstanding, once the successor is known, he can only be installed by the king-makers, who in Bali Nyonga are the Nwana, the representatives of the commoners.

THE RITUAL INSTALLATION OF THE FON

The general public knows very little about the ritual installation of the Fon, which is carried out in the depths of the Fon's palace by the Nwana. Soon after the death of the Fon occurs, the Nwanas are summoned by Gwanvoma to the palace together with leading traditional nobles known to have been confidants of the deceased monarch. Leading descendants of the royal lineage are also present. The palace is sealed by the Ngumba, making access impossible for ordinary people. At this point, the identity of the heir apparent is revealed, and, provided there is unanimity among the confidants, the heir is then "held" by his brothers and sisters, ceremonially beaten and handed over to the senior descendants of the royal lineage, Tita Nji and Tita Fonkwa. They, in turn, hand over the heir to Tita Langa, who takes him into a specially secluded room where the deceased Fon has been lying in state. Tita Langa then begins the profoundly secret ritual of installing the new Fon.

Our informants and the general public are told that at one point in the ritual, the heir supports the head of his father's corpse on his lap, a gesture meant to signify the transfer of royal mystic powers from the one to the other. The public is told that the new Fon spends three days and three nights of mourning during which he lies on plantain leaves on the floor. He may only talk with the Nwanas. During the initiation, the new Fon also undergoes the rites reserved for nobles as described above. Obviously, the secret rituals involved in installing the Fon are more elaborate than what has been described, and we can only hope that full documentation of this will be available to posterity through the diligence of those initiated persons who also happen to be enlightened. In this regard, it is pertinent to regard with caution published accounts of the ritual installation that have not been presented by eye-witnesses.

Part of the installation ceremony takes place in public. The highlights of these are the ascent of the Lela Shrine with the accompaniment of the music, the delivery of a policy speech by the new Fon, the military salute and the ceremonial sitting on the traditional throne. All these are described fully below as observed during the installation of H.R.H. Ganyonga III.

THE SUCCESSION OF H.R.H. GALEGA II BY H.R.H. GAN-YONGA III

H.R.H. Galega II died on September 18, 1985, at the Shisong Catholic Hospital, Nso, after a protracted illness. His body was returned to Bali on the same day for funeral rites and burial. Upon learning that "the fire had gone out" in Bali Nyonga, the public authorities of the Cameroon Government sent a large contingent of armed gendarmes and policemen to guard the palace and maintain the peace. A strict pass was immediately instituted, and only king-makers, distinguished nobles and members of the royal family were allowed into the palace.

Although the identity of the heir apparent was a public secret, we are told that the subdivisional officer for Bali interviewed the king-makers individually to establish the heir. H.R.H. Galega II, a man of great wisdom, had also made the task easy by leaving a legally certified "will" with the Government and other authorities. The only point of concern was that the heir-apparent, Dr. Bika'i Dohsang, was away in West Germany where he had studied and was working. He was contacted and told to come home because of his father's serious illness. Informed sources have it that he arrived at Douala on the night of 22nd September 1985 and was immediately escorted to Bali by the police. Upon arrival in Bali, he was handed to the Nwana, who had all these days been camping at the palace patiently waiting for him. As has always been the case, the ritual installation rites began in all secrecy and details are not known to us.

After the installation ceremony, the public funeral was set for September 26, 27 and 28. The 26th was the day of burial, the 27th the day of presentation of the new Fon, and the 28th, the day of mourning. Generally, in Bali tradition, the funeral of men lasts for three days and that of women for four days. We were present at the burial and presentation ceremonies and had the opportunity to see the practice of what was known in theory.

September 26th, 1985, was the day set aside for the public burial of H.R.H. Galega II. According to tradition, the deceased Fon is buried in a private ceremony, but an effigy is publicly buried to commemorate the Fon. On the morning of that day, the dance piazza, Ntan Mfon, in front of the palace, was packed full of Bali people seated according to traditional protocol. On the right of the palace gate and facing the Lela Shrine was an unadorned wooden sofa with two ivory buggies, Ntang Mfon, placed at its feet. To mark the mournful occasion, the traditional throne was not used. To the right of the gate were the Koms, who were followed immediately by the Fonte'. The princes, Bon Mfon, came next after the Fonte'. In this group of princes one could identify the late Fon's brothers, uncles and cousins. His sons and daughters, as principal mourners (Bon-Nchi) were reserved a place of honour to the left of the Wolela (Lela Shrine) facing the main palace gate.

To the left of the palace gate was the royal orchestra manned by the Tsinted and Kufat elements. Then came the Tutuwan close to the left side of the palace gate. On this solemn occasion, the two traditional emblems had been pinned near the palace gate to mark the importance of the event. Normally, these emblems come out of the palace for public display only twice yearly, at the Lela festivals in June and December. To the left of the Tutuwan were the Ngumba group dressed in flashy red tunics.

The rest of the piazza was filled with ordinary Bali folks. Everybody present had shaved their head clean and dressed themselves in white mourning garments. The royal children, in addition, had white-washed their faces as a sign of mourning. Altogether no less than 10,000 people were gathered at the piazza to do honour to the memory of H.R.H. Galega II. Dr. J.N. Foncha, former Vice-President of the defunct Federal Republic of Cameroon, Hon. Mayi-Matip Theodore, Vice-President of the National Assembly and Chief Victor Mukete were among the official dignitaries who came to witness the burial of H.R.H. Galega II and the installation of his successor.

The ceremonies started around 11 a.m. with the arrival of the Senior Divisional Officer (SDO) for Mezam, who also represented the Governor of the North West Province on this occasion. After reading a telegram of condolences from H.E. Paul Biya, President of the Republic of Cameroon, to the Bali people and the bereaved family, the SDO delivered an eulogy. He lauded H.R.H. Galega II as an illustrious son of Cameroon, a man who had fought for peace and independence of the country; a man who had inspired the economic expansion of Bali during his forty-five-year reign.

The burial rites began immediately after the SDO's speech. To spark off the event, a vanguard of the Ngumba society dressed in a flashy feather tunic known as *Mupuh*, emerged from the palace holding a club and spear in his hands. After giving the traditional military salute, Lo'ti at the Mfon's gate, he disappeared into the palace. Then two leading members of the Voma society, Tita Gwan-voma and Tita Labi, emerged from the palace, dressed in white traditional military tunics called palewa. Placing themselves respectively on the right and the left of the palace gate and facing the Lela Shrine, the two representatives of Voma started to play mournfully on a pair of double gongs, Mukoengkoeng, also known as Yaa Shu in Mubako. At this signal, the royal funeral dance known as Yaa was tuned by the Tsinted. Yaa is actually a cavalry marching song played with two drums. It was handed down from the time when the Bali army was mounted. At the sound of Yaa music, the Kufad allies joined in with their xylophones, (Ndzang Kufat).

Then the Nwana emerged from the palace gate carrying the effigy of the late Fon dressed in hand-woven royal cloth known as Ndop. The effigy was borne shoulder-high on two pillars (Gela) by Tita Musing and Tita Nyagang Kolbe, both of them members of the Nwana. Other Nwana accompanying the effigy were Monsam (Nwana-Yedla), Fofunjuh, and Tita Langa.

When the Nwana emerged from the palace with the effigy, deep emotion was stirred in the large crowd gathered at the Lela piazza. Loud sobs could be heard as men, women, and children wept at what was the final public memorial of a great man. The Nwana bore the effigy in a farewell military salute (Lo'ti), which they performed at the palace gate to the accompaniment of Yaa and Ndzang Kufat music; the sounds of ivory buggies and the beating of the royal drums, Dang-dang and Danga underscored the royal nature of the manifestation. Trailed by the traditional emblems and a mammoth crowd, the effigy was borne to its final resting place at Fomuso Hills in Jamjam quarter. Heavy bursts of gunfire accompanied by war songs continued to animate the occasion till late in the evening.

The Presentation of H.R.H. Ganyonga III to the Bali Population

Tradition requires that the ritual burial of the Fon's effigy should be followed by the public presentation of the new Fon. This took place on the 27th September 1985. The dance piazza, Ntan Mfon, was packed full in the same manner as it was on the previous day of burial.

The ceremony began at 11 a.m. when the Ngumba representative, wearing a *Mupuh* (feather tunic), came out of the palace to signal the arrival of the Fon. Then one of the Nwana in the person of Dayebga Tita Nji III came out of the palace and placed himself on the left side of the palace gate. As soon as he started to play on the double gongs or Yaa Shu, the other Nwana (eight were present) appeared stripped to the waist and holding sacred spears called Dingsoga. A mobile cow-skin tent known as *dala* or *dara* was then squeezed out of the palace gate as Yaa and Ndzang Kufat music continued to play. Responding to the music, the Nwana guided the skin tent, which was carried by the Tsinted, in a majestic march towards the Lela Shrine, where the tent was opened and the Fon H.R.H. Ganyonga III emerged from it, amidst applause, to mount the Lela Shrine. He was dressed in resplendent white robes and wore the royal headgear, Feleng, adorned with red and white feathers. The Fon then mounted and stood on the shrine guarded by the Nwana who had initiated him. Also accompanying the Fon at the shrine were two representatives of the **Kom Ngong** in the persons of **Gwanyebid** and **Gwanmusia**. **Tita Nukuna** represented the Lela society and Bangu, standing at the palace gate with the royal staff, Bang Fukang represented the Fonte.

Figure 4.3. Fon Ganyonga III in mourning garments at his ascent of the Lela Stone pyramid.

Once mounted on the Lela shrine, the Fon made his inaugural speech. Speaking through the Kom, he thanked his people for the trouble they had taken to organise the event and then pledged to fulfil his role as the Fon of Bali. He urged the people to support the national government and party and to be law-abiding. The Fon was then led to the palace gate, where he sat on the throne for a while before standing up to receive military salutes (Lo'ti), first from the **Nwana** and then from the **Tutuwan**. He then withdrew to the palace. Lela music and gun-firing continued for nearly two hours, followed by other traditional dances which lasted till late in the evening.

Figure 4.4. Ba Titanji, a close personality to V.S. Galega II. He represented the Fon on many occasions during the reign of V.S. Galega II

The public burial and presentation ceremonies clearly showed the traditional institutions in action. The leading role of the Nwana was obvious at all steps. However, they were not isolated as the Tsinted, Kom ngong, Fonte' and Sama also took part in the manifestations. In particular, the presentation ceremony was so designed as to clearly illustrate the unity of the traditional institutions in installing the Fon of Bali.

PART THREE

The Executive Branch

Soh (1978), quoting Hunt, has concluded in his study of the Bali political system that it was originally a military despotic system in which the Fon had absolute power. Accordingly, therefore, there was no deputy Fon as is the case in some tribes in the North West Province of Cameroon. This does not mean, however, that the Fon of Bali ruled single-handedly or without consulting his nobles. Every Fon since Galega I has gathered around him a "cabinet" to assist him in his daily administrative duties. Although many of the Fon's collaborators were hereditary titleholders, the formal possibility existed for the Fon to appoint capable commoners to certain key functions in the palace. The classification of the Bali system as despotic is, therefore, unjustifiable.

Constitutional Cabinet

This term, which has no equivalent in the Bali-Nyonga language, is coined as a collective name to designate those positions which the Fon must fill upon his ascent to the throne. The posts of Fomungwi, Tita Sikod, Tita Sama, Tita Nyagang (of the Lela society), Mamfon (Ganua) and Tutuwan are non-hereditary and may be renewed when the Fon takes over power.

Kah Mfomungwi or the Queen —is a titular position unique to Bali-Nyonga and absent among the other Bali tribes. It dates from the time of Nah-Nyonga, the female progenitor of the Bali kings. This position is filled by the Fon's half-sister. Kah Mfomungwi is the closest we have to a deputy Fon. She is supposed to substitute for the Fon in many of his functions. She has a compound of her own, and her "gate is inaugurated." In public ceremonies, she dresses in royal garments "with a moon design on its back" and sits on a throne close by the Fon. Because of the male-dominated character of the Bali society, Kah Mfomungwi has turned out to be more of a figurehead than a real administrative assistant to the Fon.

Tita Sikod: is the military commander of the Fon's bodyguards. He is the son of a princess (daughter of the reigning or dead Fon). Upon appointment, Tita Sikod is initiated into the Fon's inner circle of collaborators. He is an ex-officio member of the Sama group. In public ceremonies, he is responsible for the security of the Fon and is always close by him. He helps the Kom Tsinted to organise the distribution of food and gunpowder at public manifestations. When a Nkom ngong is appointed, it is Tita Sikod who takes him from the Palace gate to hand him over to the other Kom Ngong, who then publicly present him to the population gathered at the Lela Piazza.

Tita Sama: Is the modern equivalent of a property manager. He is selected from the maternal family of the late Fon and is an uncle to the ruling Fon. In Bali-Nyonga, Tita Sama is expected to take care of the Fon's business, to organise and host the funerals of the ruling Fon's wives and children. He is like a father to the Fon. He is initiated into the Bali state cult and is an ex officio member of the Sama, a group of the Lela Society. In ritual ceremonies, he occupies a place of honour and may sit on the "grass mat" or *Sadliga* usually reserved for the Fon. He enjoys the honorific title of Mo, which is a prerogative of princes and Fonte.

Tita Nyagang: Is the head of the military wing of the Lela institution. He is selected from among the descendants of the original Yani stock and initiated in the conduct of rites. He is initiated into the Bali state cult and may wear a red feather on his cap. In public ceremonies, he may substitute for the Fon in offering sacrifices. He personally leads the Flag bearers or Tutuwan in their military displays at the Lela festival. Though not of royal origin, Tita Nyagang enjoys the honorific address of Mo.

Ma Mfon (Ganua): Is the King's mother. After the funeral rites have been completed, the mother of the reigning Fon is anointed as Ma-mfon, affectionately called Kah. The Bali say she is like a King. She has her own compound and is a close adviser to the Fon.

New Elements in the Administrative Setup of Bali Nyonga

In modern times, where traditional authorities have to collaborate with national authorities, some of the hereditary title holders have proven to be technically unqualified to handle such complicated issues as collecting taxes, organising community development projects and mobilising the population in favour of certain actions of the national government. Under such conditions, Galega II modified the traditional system by introducing new posts to meet the needs of modernisation. We outline here some of the most prominent modifications ushered in during the past 40-50 years.

The Traditional Council: Originally this Council functioned only as an informal consultative body. It comprised the *Kom Kwatad* and Fonte' and some senior Tsinted. Usually, the Fon consulted each group separately and only convened them in a plenary session to announce decisions. There was no system allowing for organised debate over issues, and a consensus was usually reached only after intense private consultations. Because of their increasing importance and the democratisation of the society as a whole, the Sama, Nwana, Bon Mfon (royal children) and Yefana (the youths) were included in a reorganised traditional Council during the reign of H.R.H. Galega II. Another important modification was to select from the existing traditional groups two persons to sit on the **Traditional Executive Council** when it was called upon to discuss matters with national administrative authorities. During such meetings, the Fon could be represented by a representative (see below). Although the name was not given to it, this restricted traditional Council acted as an executive body of the larger Council, comprising all the titular nobles.

The inclusion of *Bon Mfon* and *Yefana* in the traditional Council is a welcome departure from what obtained in the past, where the informal consultative group on which the Fon relied for advice comprised mainly Kom, Tsinted and Fonte'. The inclusion of the Sama and Nwana into the traditional Council is also a recent development, which had its roots during the reign of Fonyonga II and became a permanent feature during the reign of Galega II.

The Fon's Representative: This position grew out of necessity during the reigns of H.R.H. Galega II. As a parliamentarian and member of the West Cameroon House of Chiefs, H.R.H. Galega II was often out of Bali and it became necessary under these circumstances to have someone available to decide on immediate issues and to receive visiting officials of the national government. During the reign of Galega II, such a post devolved on Dayebga Tita Nji III. In his analysis of the Bali Political System, Aletum, speaks of the "Titanji Institution" as a kind of coordinator of the traditional institutions who is directly responsible to the Fon. He traces this "institution" back to the time of Galega I who introduced it to honour his eldest son (Aletum & Fonyuy, 1985).

The 'Minister' of Palace Affairs: We have coined this term, which does not exist in the original Bali vocabulary, to designate one of those palace functions that evolved out of practical need and has become a permanent feature of the Bali traditional set-up. The titular post of Tita Sama was originally designed to provide a kind of economic manager to care for the personal business of the Fon. During the reign of the personally wealthy Fonyonga II, it turned out that this function was too complicated to be performed by one person. Fonyonga II owned several herds of cattle, sheep and goats as well as extensive maize farms and raffia palm bushes. To his wealth was added a very large immediate family numbering up to between 300 and 400. The need arose then to designate somebody to follow up matters relating to the management of his property and family. This post first went to Tita Fokum, who by virtue of his personal dynamism, quickly converted this position to one of great influence. At the death of Fonyonga II the position passed on to Tita Kehdinga, the half-brother of H.R.H. Galega II. When Tita Kehdinga died in the mid-fifties, the position then passed on to Tita Nukuna. Tita Nukuna, among his other duties, is in charge of giving princesses in marriage, and in a general way, is responsible for the internal administration of the palace. Tita Nukuna is a member of the Sama group of the Lela institution.

Figure 4.5. Tita Nukuna Fonyonga. He was in charge of palace administration during the reign of V.S. Galega II.

The Fon's Secretary: Very often, the Fon of Bali may co-opt individuals with special abilities to perform specific duties even though they may not be title holders. In such cases, they may be nominally assimilated into the ranks of Tsinted. A particular case in point is the post of the Fon's secretary, which in recent times has been occupied by such individuals as the late Mr. Wilfred Dook, the late Mr. Alfred Daiga (later a parliamentarian in the West Cameroon House of Assembly), Vincent Nteh and presently Ndanjong. Though these individuals were not originally titular nobles in Bali, through association with the palace, they became very influential figures.

Figure 4.6. A cross section of the population at the Bali Nyonga Palace Plaza during the funeral of V.S. Galega II.

CONCLUDING REMARKS

Analysing the Bali Traditional political system, Soh (1978) identified social mobility as a factor that satisfied the ambitions of non-royals, who, in spite of their humble birth, could attain the status of nobility on merit through the Fon's appointment. Social mobility can thus be seen as a factor which facilitated the assimilation of other ethnic groups into Bali Nyonga and thereby favoured its internal cohesion. In this regard, it is worthwhile noting that the traditional system of Bali Nyonga grew out of the need to reconstruct the defunct Chamba system that existed before the split at Bafu-Fondong, and at the same time, accommodate the new ethnic groups that had joined Bali Nyonga during their migration to the present settlement.

In the system that emerged the Fon remained the central figure, now shared his authority with such hereditary title holders like Fonte', Kom Kwatad, Ba-Nwana etc., whom he could not simply dismiss from office without undermining his legitimacy. Lela and Voma, which started as cults, became thoroughly politicised as they incorporated many of the decision-makers and title-holders. However, this mixture of religion and politics is not unique to Bali Nyonga.

The Bali Nyonga system of government cannot, in our opinion, be equated to any modern system. Although it had the characteristics of military despotism, with the Fon as the central figure, it also had aspects of a representative government with titleholders drawn from different social groups of the community. By giving the Fon the free hand to appoint and dismiss from office, the system displayed characteristics of cabinet government.

The durability of the Bali Nyonga system is supported by its ability to have survived not only the pre-colonial and colonial eras, but to remain viable even within the context of post-colonial independent Cameroon. This and other traditional African systems of government are worthy of further study for possible hints in our search for stable forms of government in post-independent Africa.

GLOSSARY

- **Ba'ni** (Mubako[1]): Plural form of the word Yani, meaning horse rider. This word is a precursor of the word Bali, which designates the Subdivision inhabited by the Chamba elements of the North West Province.
- **Bati**: Bamileke elements who joined the Bali before and after their occupation of the present site at Bali Nyonga. The Bali adopted their language. Mungaka, for military purposes. Subsequently, Mungaka replaced the original

1 Mn= Mungaka, Mb=Mubako

Bali language, Mubako, as the language of administration and commerce.

- **Bon Mfon** (Mn): Princes and Princesses. This term is also used to designate other relatives of the Fon, particularly those whose descent from the royal family is patrilineal.
- **Bon Nchi** (Mn): Orphans.
- **Dingsoga** (Mb): A wooden staff with a metallic shoe used in Voma rituals. Only senior members of the Voma and Lela cults may own one of these.
- **Dola** (Mb): A building in a secluded area where Voma Society holds its meetings.
- **Feleng** (Mn): A traditional cap worn as a mark of royalty and of decoration. It is the Bali equivalent of a crown.
- **Fon**: Popular version of the word *Mfon* (Mn) meaning King or National Ruler.
- **Fonte'** (Mn): Traditional dignitaries holding the rank of a sub-chief.
- **Fonyonga II**: Fon of Bali from 1901–1940.
- **Galega** (Mb): "King of the House." This name has been taken by two monarchs of Bali Nyonga i.e. Galega I who ruled Bali until 1901 and Galega II who ruled Bali from 1940–1985.
- **Goela (Gela)** (Mb): A stretcher made of two wooden poles and decorated with hand-woven cloth used in the burial of royalty.
- **Gwe (Gwei)** (Mb): An agent or jester associated with the military wing of the Lela Cult.
- **Kah** (Mb): Grandmother. Honorific title of the Queen-Mother or Queen. Also used in ordinary speech to mean grandmother.
- **Kefad** (Kufat) (Mb): One of the tribes that was assimilated into Bali during the reign of Gawolbe I.
- **Kom** (Mn): A titular noble with the rank of a cabinet officer

in the court of the Fon of Bali. Kom Ngong – ministers of state. (Nkom singular, Kom plural).

- **Lekashua / Lekasiwaa:** Descendants of female relatives. Also used as a name for the smallest of the Lela flutes.
- **Lela** (Mb): A Bali cult that holds annual festivals in June and December. Also used to designate the songs and flutes used during the festival.
- **Le'ti** (Mn): A traditional military dance performed with weapons to the tune of war songs, and often used as a form of salute during public manifestations like Lela and the funerals of men.
- **Mo** (Mn): Honorific answer to Princes and sub-chiefs. It translates approximately to "Yes, Your Honour." The corresponding honorific title reserved from Mo is Ndey. The Mfon alone is answered Chabifo or Mbe.
- **Mupuh** (Mb): A feathered tunic with a cloth mask used by Ngumba in their public ceremonies. One who wears such a dress.
- **Mukengkeng** (**Mukoengkoeng**) (Mn): Metallic double-gong used by the Ngumba and other societies to summon members. Also used as a musical piece.
- **Musing** (Mn): Bird (literally "Ma Pob Musung" = Ma way Musung = Ma Pob Bunga). All these expressions refer to an initiation rite through which nobles and the Fon must undergo in order to become full members of the Voma and Lela societies. Initiated persons are allowed to wear a decorative red turaco feather as a sign of distinction.
- **Nyagang** (Mb): One who mixes medicines, a pharmacist. A traditional title in the Lela and Voma cults.
- **Nah Nyonga** (Mb): Legendary female progenitor of the Fons of Bali Nyonga. Daughter of Gawolbe I.
- **Ndop** (Mn): Handwoven cloth decorated with blue and white designs reserved for royalty.

- **Ngumba** (Mb): A regulatory fraternity equivalent to the Kwifon in Tikar chiefdoms, charged with enforcing the decisions of the Fon.
- **Nketi** (Mn): Deputy. Nketi Mfon – Deputy chief. A titular position among some chiefdoms of the North West Province. No such title exists in Bali Nyonga.
- **Ntan Mfon** (Mn): The Mfon's dance plaza – an open circular courtyard in front of the Fon's palace in Bali Nyonga. The Lela Shrine (Wolela) is located in this piazza, which is also the scene of many traditional gatherings, e.g., the traditional court presided over by Kom Ngong.
- **Ntang Mfon** (Mn): The Fon's ivory trumpet used in traditional ceremonies to summon the population. It is a prerogative of the royalty to have this trumpet sounded at their funerals.
- **Nwana** (mb): Guard, Rain or Spirit (literal trans.) A leading title holder among the members of the Voma cult. Together, the Nwana constitute the group of Kingmakers, charged with anointing, initiating and presenting the Fon to the population. There were originally 7 Nwana, all of them drawn from non-royal elements. Today, there are 13.
- **Sadliga** (Mb): Kay Sadliga. Grass mat used by the Mfon instead of the throne during solemn meetings of the Lela and Voma societies. Tita Sama may sit on one such mat as well.
- **Sama** (Mb): Titular Member of the Lela cult. Also used as the name of twins.
- **Tita** (Mb): Prince, commander, or group leader. This title is usually attributed to Princes who have come of age and built their own compounds. A limited number of meritorious individuals may be given this title as well, e.g. Kom Tsinted or the Kom Ba'ni.
- **Tsinted** (Mn): A miscellaneous group of courtiers and

servants with special duties at the Mfon's palace. Nchinted (singular). Tsinted (plural). One who sojourns at the palace (literal translation).

- **Tikwanga** (Mb): Ward-head. Title holder in the Voma Society.
- **Tutuwan (Tutunwan)** (mb): Guard of the Flag (literal translation). One of the titular standard bearers associated with the military wing of the Lela Society. Also used to designate the flags or standards themselves.
- **Voma** (Mb): A fertility cult of the Bali chiefdoms, in charge of fighting evil spirits and initiating the Fon and other title holders. Holds two annual demonstrations in January-February and in October. Also used to designate the sacred objects of divination used during Voma Society celebrations. **Vomlangu** = first fruits' Voma celebrated in January-February. **Voma** is also a common name given to male children born during the **Voma** festival.
- **Vomdzaana** (Mb): The historical antecedent of the **Ngumba** group, now defunct in Bali Nyonga, its functions have been assimilated into other traditional groups, e.g. the Ngumba and Voma societies.
- **Vom-Keina** (Mb): Voma's wives (literal trans.). Women choristers of the Voma society.
- **Vomnunga** (Mb): Ceremonial closing of the Voma season in January or February.
- **Wolela (Mn):** A stone pyramid in the Fon's dance piazza representing the Lela Shrine.
- **Yaa (Mb):** Horse (literal trans.). Also used to designate a royal dance of the original cavalry of the now disbanded Bali army. The Yaa music is used to initiate the funerals of male members of the nobility (Princes and other titular nobles).
- **Yaa Shu** (Mb): Double gongs played by the Nwana at the

funerals of important dignitaries.

- **Yani** (Mb): Horse rider (literal trans.). Also used to designate the original Bali elements from Chamba. Yani (singular), Ba'ni (plural).

BIBLIOGRAPHY

Aletum, T. M., & Fonyuy, F. C. (1985). *The traditional political institutions of Bali-Nyonga and their contributions to modern polities in Cameroon.*

Chilver, E. M. (1966). *Zintgraff's exploration in Bamenda, Adamawa and the Benue Lands, 1889-1892.* Government Printing Press.

Green, M. (1982). *Through the year in Africa.* Batsford Academic and Education Ltd.

Kaberry, P. M., & Chilver, E. M. (1961). An outline of the traditional political system of Bali Nyonga, Southern Cameroons. *Africa, 31*, 355–371.

Ndangam, A. F., & Nwana, E. M. (n.d.). *Portrait of their royal highness, Galega I, Fonyonga II and Galega II.* (Mimeographed document).

Nwana, E. M. (1986). *The past as perceived by the Bali Nyonga people of Cameroon.* Manuscript prepared for the World Archaeological Congress, Southampton and London.

Soh, B. P. (1978). *A study of Bali Nyonga: History and the Lela cult.* Unpublished manuscript, Centre de Recherches de la Literature Traditionnelle, O.N.A.R.E.S.T.

5

The Mungaka Language
Its Development, Spread, and Use

Adolf Sema Lima

It is a truism that the identity and hallmark of a people is their culture. Culture, in a nutshell, implies the sum total of the knowledge, beliefs, and practices of a people, all of which portray their civilisation, their way of life. A sine qua non for the fulfilment of all this is language, one of man's greatest gifts, which, like the air around him, is all too often taken for granted, but without which he cannot carry out his multifarious life's experiences.

So complex is the concept of language that views on it vary considerably. For Emerson, language is a city to the building of which every human being brought a stone. W.F. Mackey (1965:3) in his review of the diversity of opinions about language sums up the multi-dimensional characteristics of it as follows: "To the philosopher, language may be an instrument of thought; to the sociologist, a form of behaviour; to the psychologist, a cloudy window through which he glimpses the workings of the mind; to the logician it may be calculus; to the engineer, a series of physical events; to the statistician, a selection by choice and chance; to the linguist, a system of arbitrary signs." Definitions of language by linguists are numerous and varied, but they all converge on the end-product of it, which is meaning in usage, for this is what makes man distinct from beast. It can be deduced from the foregoing that language is the vehicle of all culture. It therefore invariably plays a preponderant role in the manner in which the way of life of a people is ordered, effected, and passed from one generation to another. In light of this, it is the aim of this article to trace the origin of Mungaka as well as examine to some extent some aspects of the development, spread, and use of the language as a powerful vehicle with which the Bali culture is exercised, preserved, and propagated.

NOMENCLATURE

Mungaka

Mungaka is the language of the Bali Nyonga people, found in the Bali Subdivision in the Mezam Division of the North West Province. Bali Nyonga constitutes one of many groups of Chamba origin to be found mostly in the North West Province. All other groups (apart from the Bali Nyonga) speak closely related varieties of a language known as Mubako, about which mention will be made subsequently. Mungaka [mungaka] literally means "I say," a characteristic feature of the nomenclature of many a language of the North West Province such as Moghamo [mo ghamo] "I say"; Monemo [mo nemo] "I say"; La'mbo [La' mbo] "I say"; for the languages of the people of Moghamo and Meta of Momo Division and Kedjom (Babanki) of Mezam Division (as an alternative form of Ga'a Kedjom) respectively. In the specific case of Mungaka, a morphemic synthesis of the name is imperative. Mu + nga + ka [mu + nga + ka] make up the composite parts (morphemes) of the name of the language.

mu = 'me'
nga = 'I say' (conjugated)
ka = 'affirmative particle'

Mungaka, therefore, strictly speaking, literally means 'Me, I say'. The analysis reveals a double subject (pronoun) morpheme since the form 'Ngaka' by itself means 'I say', for 'n', i.e., the nasal /n/ represents an assimilated form of 'mu'. Ndangam (1972:3) rightly points out that Ngaka is another form of the name of the language. However it must be made clear that this abbreviated form is in addition used in speech as a signal as when a speaker calls on his interlocutor when the former insistently draws the attention of the latter to the fact that he is speaking to him, in which case he is required to answer 'yes' i.e., /n/ as assurance that he is attentively listening and participating. The form Mungaka is therefore reserved for the name of the language, especially in formal usage.

Bali, Ba'ni...

Although Mungaka is the rightful name of the language, other forms of it can be unravelled from the speech of many speakers of the language, including some native speakers. One such usage is 'Bali'. To refer to Mungaka as Bali is a misnomer because it is misleading, as it creates confusion between the name of the village, its people, and their language. This tendency probably derives from the descriptive name "Tsu Ba'ni" in Mungaka, which literally means "Talk (of the) Bali," or "Language Bali," i.e., Bali language—a rather universal descriptive name to all languages, e.g., the English language, the Japanese language, the Chinese language, etc. Ba'ni in this appellation is the original native version of the now anglicised authentic form 'Bali', which dates from the colonial period when the colonial pathfinders, who found it difficult to articulate the exotic sounds in the African names they were faced with, proceeded to effect phonological adaptations and smoothing of sorts. On the issue of the name of the people itself, Ndangam (op. cit.) points out that the name of the tribe is, like the complexity of the language situation, confusing since the names Ba'ni, Bali Nyonga, Banyonga, and Nyongneba all refer to one and the same people, as can be found in various articles and books on the Bali people. No wonder, therefore, that earlier writers (journalists, historians, sociologists, etc.) indiscriminately used unorthodox names such as Bali and Ba'ni to refer to both people and language. A typical example of this is recorded in a Church history publication in Mungaka in which the author, Rev. Dr. Adolf Vielhauer (1944), explains the confusion in the name of the language between the Bali language and Mungaka, finally settling on Mungaka instead of the former, which he had earlier used. Ndangam (1972:4) argues in his conclusion on the same issue that Vielhauer's principal reason for preferring religious (Bali being geographically more limited than Mungaka which refers to myriads of speakers of it beyond the borders of Bali and therefore more general as the Christian message which is not limited to the Jews but also to the Gentiles and all the earth) rather than a conclusion which is obvious from Vielhauer's own explanation.

HISTORICAL PERSPECTIVE

Mungaka is, in fact, not the original language of the Bali Nyonga people. A review of the history of the Balis by Gwanfogbe shows that they came from Chamba, having probably escaped from a protracted drought and other climatic hazards, and relentlessly fought their way battle after battle to their present sites, where for a long time, they were further subjected to sporadic survival-of-the-fittest upheavals, all of which they must have surmounted to merit their present geographical location. Ndifontah's more detailed study (1988) throws more light on the origin, movements, contacts, and final settlement of the Balis at their present sites.

It is interesting to note that up until the death of Gawolbe, (the leader of the Balis then) at the major battle of Bafu-Fundong near Djuitisa in Dschang (as will be explained later), all the Bali groups were one people, under one monarch, united by one purpose and one culture. Above all, they spoke the original form of Mubako, it being evident that contemporary Mubako has undergone and continues to undergo various linguistic transformations.

Gawolbe's tragic death marked a turning point in the union of the Chamba group, and in a way it can be argued that it was the event that later triggered off the birth of Mungaka, for as Gwanfogbe puts it, if Gawolbe's heir-apparent, Gangsin, had been powerful and competent, he would have been able to weld together the Chamba people and establish a strong and united Kingship, as there were several able postulants to the throne. The unpleasant result was a split into the well-known seven Balis — Bali Muti, Bali Kontan, Bali Kumbat, Bali Gasu (Gashu), Bali Gangsin, Bali Gham, and Bali Nyonga respectively. It is to be noted that Bali Kontan was later assimilated by the Bali Nyonga group, and this explains why no mention is made about them anymore. The Bali Nyonga group is the only one of all the groups that acquired a totally different language other than the original one. Further adventures were thereafter to play a major role in the coming into being of Mungaka.

Theories of the Origin of Mungaka

Several theories claim to explain the curious question of the origin of Mungaka.

The Invention Theory

One rather simplistic theory based on oral tradition holds that Mungaka was 'invented' long after the settlement at the present site of Bali Nyonga. It is claimed that this came as a result of the arrival of many foreigners into the Bali group, a situation which hampered easy communication between the new arrivals and the aborigines. The need for a common code as a unifying factor amongst peoples of different origins arose. This, according to the 'invention' theory, led to the spontaneous invention of a language.

Such a theory is far from being plausible, as it leaves many crucial questions unanswered. Mungaka is a natural language, not an Esperanto. The proofs for this are manifold. It could therefore not have been 'invented'.

The Midi of a Gift

Another theory, which is in fact a myth (and therefore far from being credible), is the belief that Mungaka was a ready-made package gift to the people from the monarch of the time (Nyongpasi), who in turn is believed to have mysteriously acquired it from some divine source. Like the other incredible theory, this too is as good as the old wife's tale. What is, however, remarkable about this legendary theory is the pointer to the royal authority as the authentic source and therefore the custodian of language, as the embodiment of culture. It is interesting to note that to date, it is strongly held in Bali that the monarch is the focus of the purity of the language, and indeed he is, although this has no cause-and-effect relationship with the 'ready-made package gift' theory mentioned above.

It must, however, be stated in categorical terms that language is no artifact that can simply be handed over to a beneficiary in its polished and ready-to-use form. All languages have an evolutionary history that can adequately explain their diachronic and synchronic development. And Mungaka is no exception to the rule.

The Historical and Evolutionary Theory

There is a more plausible theory of the origin of Mungaka. Historically speaking, the Bali Chamba raiders are said to have settled for quite a long while in the Bamum (Bamoun) and Bati (Ti or Pati) neighbourhood during which period they fought with each of these tribes. Before their arrival, the two tribes had, however, constantly been at war. The Chambas sought in vain to subjugate the Bamums, but managed to assimilate some of the Batis whom they had easily subjugated and with whom they had a better relationship into their group as they moved further southwards. It can already be posited that this early contact between the Chamba and both the Bati and Bamum must have been instrumental in initiating the former into the language of the latter. Thus, when the whole Chamba group moved southwards from the Bati region, they took the Bati language with them.

It is crucial at this point to draw attention to the linguistic affinity that exists between Mungaka and the Bati language. There is evidence that the latter is the mother base of the former. The Bati and Bamum languages share linguistic similarities. Mungaka and Bamum, too, have much in common. It is therefore syllogistic to conclude that Mungaka is the product of Bati and Bamum, although by no means the offshoot of the two only. The casual interaction between the Bati and Chamba mentioned above cannot, however, adequately account for the linguistic affinity between the two languages or partial adoption of the Bati language by the Bali Nyonga. Another contact took place subsequently.

Following the split of the Chamba group after the death of Gawolbe, the Bali Nyonga group under the leadership of Nyongpasi migrated back to the environs of Bamum where they must have renewed relations with the Bati, who, according to Gwanfogbe (op. cit.), "were enemies to or recalcitrant subjects of the Bamum." It is not known for how long they must have been there, but they must likely have spent a much longer time there, thus intensifying their linguistic interaction. It was during this period that they closely observed the Bati and Bamum tribes as belligerent and even witnessed some of the carnage resulting from their conflicts. Testimony of these conflicts is contained in the oral literature of the Bali Nyonga. A typical example is a well-known ballad entitled 'Nkang mbab...' The ballad ends with the lines:

> "Bati ka wad Bamum e
> Bamum ka wad Bati e"

Which means:

> "The Bati people slaughtered the Bamum

The Bamum (people) slaughtered the Bati."

This is an eyewitness account of a carnage which they must have witnessed. Gwanfogbe points out that it is not certain why they finally left Bati. He, however, suggests that "an attempted allied war with the Bati against the Bamum must have failed to yield them dividends." Oral sources suggest that the Bali Nyonga left Bati because they were rather uncomfortable there, as they were geographically sandwiched between the Bamum and Bati and were therefore not as free as they wanted to be. Besides, the land area where they settled temporarily was grossly insufficient. Also, they could hardly exert much influence on their neighbours. When finally, they left, they took along with them a sizeable number of the Bati people whose confidence and sympathy they had won to their present site. This long-lived coexistence with the Bati must have had a significant linguistic influence from the Bati language on the Bali Nyonga.

It is clear that during the first and casual contact of the Bali Chamba group and the Bati, the former was large and overwhelming. During the second contact, the Bali Nyonga group was now a smaller group (since the large group had split), less influential linguistically-speaking and otherwise. It was probably for this reason that this small Bali Nyonga group was easily influenced by the language of the majority. It is a well-known fact that when two languages come into contact, the language with the greater majority of speakers takes the upper hand. This long coexistence with the Bati must have had a great linguistic impact on the Bali people.

It is also known that in the course of their march to the present site, they got in touch with other smaller groups of people, elements of whom were incorporated into their group. This perhaps explains why it is often said that Bali Nyonga is a very heterogeneous tribe. In fact, many families can still trace their ancestry to some sources foreign to Chamba origin, such as Tikali, Buti, Bati, etc. However, it is known that the Bati group did not settle in Bali Nyonga forever. They finally left Bali Nyonga after a long stay with the Bali Nyonga people at the present site. It is suggested (Buea Archives File No. Ab 1943/38 entitled Bali Language) that "the Bati left Bali on the 5th November 1911 when they were driven out as a result of trouble with their posts and they went back and settled amongst the Bamums on the right bank of the River Nun in Bati-Kali and Babuti." Bali oral tradition holds that the Bati left on their own accord and that as cunning as they were, they actually tricked the Balis on the day they left by warning that it was forbidden for anybody to come out of his house on that day because their religious priests were scheduled to walk the streets in an attempt to exorcise evil spirits from the land. When by evening, the Balis got out of their houses, they found that the Batis had departed contrary to the desires of the former. They had, however, left behind not only a handful of die-hards who were willing to settle permanently but also the early beginnings of today's Mungaka.

Incipient Mungaka

It can be deduced that incipient Mungaka was a sort of pidginized form of language derived from a fusion of the Bati and Bamum languages, as well as some Bamileke languages, such as Dschang, and other related languages with which the Balis also had casual contact. It must be asserted that at this incipient stage of their history, both Mubako and Mungaka existed side by side, for the change from Mubako to Mungaka was not sudden but gradual. This state of indigenous language — bilingualism must have existed for a long time, for as Ndangam (1972:5) put it, "... by 1889 when the German explorer Zintgraff arrived Bali Nyonga, Mubako survived only as a court language." This confirms the fact that it had earlier survived as a language of active daily use for a pretty long time before being relegated to the background for occasional use. Today, its use is a lot more restricted- to more specialized domains and by no more than a handful of Mungaka native-speakers. Mubako gave way, therefore very gradually, to Mungaka.

The Mungaka name for 'horse' is Nyam Ba'ni /nyàm bà'nì/, an expression which literally means 'animal Bali', i.e., Bali animal. It is very probable that this appellation first came from the Bati and or Bamum who acknowledged the early Chamba people as horsemen. It is doubtful that the Bali Chamba, who are said to have introduced the horse in the southern part of the country, gave the name themselves, although they were surprised to discover, as they marched southwards on horseback, that the horse was a novelty to the people. Those early Bati people called it 'Nyam Bare.' By analogy, the Bali people have come to name many other objects on the basis of this possessive nomenclature, e.g., a species of potatoes, a species of groundnuts, etc., although it is doubtful that they were the first to introduce them in their environments.

Further development of early Mungaka took place in such a way that its pattern of development and expansion can be said to be coterminous with, the political expansion of the tribe as well, for as it has already been pointed out, its people and language (Mungaka) represent a quasi-microcosm of the peoples, and languages in the Grassfields region of Cameroon, all of which have now been well blended into a homogeneous whole.

Finally, it must perhaps be mentioned that as to why, of all the existing Bali Chamba groups, only the Bali Nyonga, to the best of our knowledge, is known to have evolved another language, almost to the abandonment or even extinction of Mubako (except as a classical language), remains somewhat of a conundrum to many. It is all the more so when one figures out that in the course of their own adventures, the other groups, too, came in contact with other languages that might well have influenced and occasioned similar changes in their language as well. One thing is certain, namely, that the 'birth' of Mungaka around 1830 vindicates the obvious observation that when several languages cohabit for some time, socio-political pressures may impose a 'survival-of-the-fittest' option on the preference or choice of one over the other. It is, besides, significant to note that the coming into being of Mungaka, which is the ultimate result of a hybridization process from the parent languages from which it took its inspiration, only helped to add to the already long list of languages in Cameroon.

TYPOLOGICAL CLASSIFICATION

Bantoid–Bantu

Malcolm Guthrie et al. (1956) classified Mungaka typologically as a Bantoid language. Greenberg (1963) later classified it as a language of the semi-Bantu type, but not as a Bantu language proper. Classifications of this type are, of course, based on some formal criteria which have to do with the analysis of formal levels, such as lexis and grammar. Chilver et al., writing even more recently in the fifties, preferred to classify Mungaka as a Bantoid language. There is great similarity between Bantoid and Bantu, and the linguistic area of difference is, to our intent and purpose, minimal.

In his review, Ndangam (1972:8) examines yet another dimension of Mungaka classification. He suggests that Mungaka is both 'isolating' and 'agglutinating'. It is isolating because it makes no use of inflexion, whether internal or external, and most words are monosyllabic, consisting of an open syllable, i.e., (C + V) or consonant combination plus 'vowel (CC + V). Similarly, it is agglutinating because it has some verbal elements which qualify it for such a classification.

It appears that classifications according to types, such as isolating, agglutinating, inflecting, and incorporating, have become obsolete. However, A.N. Tucker has observed that for African languages, such classifications may still be of value in synchronic analysis. The inconvenience of this approach is that it tends to classify the same language into different types, thereby making the classification a matter of degree rather than of absolute categories. For instance, English is agglutinating, inflexional and isolating at the same time because it exhibits characteristics of each. Mungaka, in the same vein, is clearly agglutinating and isolating and might well fit into yet another classificatory category.

Koenig et al. (1983:29), in their classification of Cameroon Home Languages, classify Mungaka as a subtype under Grassfield Bantu. Under this subtype, they include Mungaka, Bamum and Baba I. Bati, as such does not feature in the classification at least under this name, although Baba I and Bati are known to share great affinity. The reason is perhaps because their classification is based specifically on data obtained from a survey of language usage in the urban centre in Cameroon, and Bati as such might not have surfaced. Their classification is an attempt to update the grouping of Cameroon Home Languages into major languages and dialects, according to the three families known as Nilo-Saharan, Afro-Asiatic, and Niger-Congo (Greenberg, 1966). Koening et al. sought to use mutual intelligibility parameters, although with caution. In their classification, Mungaka falls within the Niger-Congo (i.e., Congo-Kordofanian) and is considered one of the 123 major home languages in Cameroon (op. cit., 1983:23).

It can be concluded from the various classifications that Mungaka belongs to the Bantu/Bantoid group. It is obvious from the classification by Koenig et al. that it constitutes a separate subclass from Mubako of the Bali Kumbat, Bali Gham and Bali Gashu groups with which Bali Nyonga has a common history, but not now a common language. It is also quite pertinent to group it with Baba and Bamum on the basis of intelligibility. To this, should be added also Bati. It is equally significant to note that, despite its relatively short-lived existence as a language, Mungaka is not only one of the major languages of Cameroon, but also one of the more widely spoken languages.

MUNGAKA-SPEAKERS

Native Speakers

Firstly, Mungaka is spoken as a mother tongue by the Bali Nyonga people resident at home and abroad. In this respect, it is (pending statistics from the recent National Census, conducted from April 10th to 24th) not easy to assess the numerical strength of native speakers with accuracy. The population figure for Bali Nyonga in the 1953 census was 18,277. Thirty-four years later, it may be modest to estimate it at slightly over 40,000 to 45,000. These would be native speakers proper of Mungaka.

Of this number, a small percentage is comprised of the Bawock, Bohsah, and Mbufung groups, all of whom are integral parts of Bali, although they are composed of much later settlers. These three sub-groups display greater linguistic flexibility, in addition to Mungaka, they also use other minor languages (in relation to a more widely spoken Mungaka). These are the Bawock language, which is itself a dialect of Bangante, and the Moghamo dialects, respectively. This status quo enables these subgroups in Bali to enjoy the status of home-language bilinguals while still being considered in varying degrees as native-speakers of Mungaka

Lingua Franca–Mungakaphone

Outside of Bali Nyonga, Mungaka has been and continues to be spoken in the North West Province as a language of wider communication. Several analysts (Ndangam 1972, Lima 1973, Nti 1973, etc.) have variously referred to and described Mungaka as a lingua franca, arguing that for long it enjoyed and still enjoys the same status as Duala, Ewondo, Fulfulde and Pidgin-English, which in their own rights too are lingua franca. Nti posited the label *Mungakaphone*, an extrapolation of similar labels such as anglophone, francophone, and arabophone, respectively, which are extensively current in the literature of linguistics, to account for the role played by Mungaka in the North West Province. For him, *Mungakaphone* implies and includes non-native speakers from all areas where Mungaka is and was actively used, i.e., spoken or understood. The term should actually be understood to include both native and non-native speakers, who use Mungaka.

This stems from the well-known fact that Mungaka was established as the language of the Basel Mission Church (now the Presbyterian Church in Cameroon) by Swiss German Missionaries from Basel upon their arrival in Cameroon in 1903. Thereafter, it served as the official language in religious matters in North West Province (then, the Grassfields Region of Southern Cameroons), just as Duala in the Coastal region, as this was consonant with the philosophy of the Church to operate in the people's own languages. This situation led to both the extensive and intensive use of Mungaka, as it was not only the language of Church affairs but also, unsurprisingly, secular interactions. It is even remarkable that North Westerners resident in the coastal region, to some extent tended to, and still tend to use Mungaka as a unifying language/factor and for other personal transactions.

It was not until recently that, even without any overt Church declarations abolishing the official use of Mungaka in Church services, many local Church leaders, for purely pragmatic reasons, began to readjust to other local languages. Even so, Bible texts are still read out in Mungaka in some cases. Alternatively, they are read out in English, or simultaneously in different vernaculars, a situation that, in the latter case, is one that cardinal Church leaders hesitate to approve of, because there is the risk that Bible passages may be misinterpreted in the process. By and large, the Church hymnal in Mungaka is still popularly in use in many congregations. Also, Mungaka choirs remain a dominant feature of choral music in many rural Church congregations, while at best, they are in keen competition with English-language choirs in congregations in urban centres.

Non-native speakers of Mungaka can be identified by their foreign accents and their formal approach to the language in both formal and informal contexts. Like the anglophone speaker of English who tends to resist gradations such as weak forms, elisions and assimilations, Mungakaphones, too, reveal a tendency to resist several aspects of gradation, such as elisions and other contracted forms in spoken Mungaka.

LINGUISTIC CHARACTERISTICS

Like all other languages, Mungaka is characterised by a number of distinguishing linguistic features. Two of them will be briefly discussed here. These are sound segments and tone, both of which constitute the sound system (phonology) of the language.

Phonology–Sound Segments

Attempts have been made by several analysts (Ndangam 1972; Nti 1973; Lima 1974) and earlier writers (Archives on Bali Language, Buea 1943), amongst others, to give a phonological description of both consonants and vowels of Mungaka. Also, the early missionaries who ultimately embarked on the codification of the language started off with studies in this area. It was most probably on the basis of their findings that they concluded that Mungaka was a simple enough language to work on as a good-enough tool for their evangelisation in the North West Province. Some disparity may be noticed in the presentation of the data in the findings by the different authors, but these are clearly minimal. A few differences, for instance, in the different inventories can be explained in terms of the acceptance of some labialized consonants as integral consonants by one analyst and as consonant clusters by others, etc. Similarly, some differences in the classification of vowels may be merely due to degrees of detail in presentation.

Our present study reveals the following findings and classifications:

Consonants

Mungaka makes use of 20 distinctive consonants of primary articulation. Six of these have the possibility of being labialized, a tendency which has tended in the works of the analysts (mentioned above) to swell the number of consonants to upwards of 27 or 28. The following is a list of the consonants and their distribution in actual usage in words.

Table 5.1. The Consonants of Mungaka

Sound	Initial Position	Medial Position	Final Position
/p/	pad (push)	lipo (type of banana)	—
/b/	ba (father)	iba (two)	ndab (house)
/t/	to (to come)	γemti (help, to help)	—
/d/	do (grandfather)	ndon (woe, ill luck)	Nkad (a visit) wad (to cut)
/k/	kan (fatigue)	ndzika (thanks)	—
/g/	gib (to doubt)	ngam (conversation)	gag (go off hand, morals)
/ts/	Tsi (to sit, spy)	Foncham (a day of the week)	—
/dz/	dzid (to walk)	mandzi (road, the way)	—
/h/	Han (superlative of whiteness)	—	—
/f/	Fan (to mistake	Ifom (eight)	—
/v/	Vin (roofing)	Vava (onomatopoeia for waterfall)	—
/s/	So (hoe)	Sisi (black)	—

Sound	Initial Position	Medial Position	Final Position
/γ/	γan (thief)	γuγa (butterfly)	—
/m/	Mun (a human being)	Bumu' (wood ash)	Sam (to hold)
/na/	Na (mother)	Ndani (clean)	Nkan (monkey)
/ń/	ńum (the sun, a clock)	Muńi (cutlass)	—
/ṅ/	ṅkwin (firewood)	ṅguṅgan (ant)	ŋgaŋ (no)
/l/	Lab (to beat)	Lili (mosquito)	—
/w/	Wo (stone)	Buwi (women)	—
/j/	Yemti (to help, help)	Mbiyaṅ (groundnuts)	—

NB: — = zero occurrence.
NB: /ts/ is almost identical with /ts/, /dz/ is also identical with /dz/ /h/ rarely occurs in Mungaka, except in some idiosyncratic interjections, e.g., he! Ha! Ho!

Table 5.2.

	Bilabial	Labiodental	Alveolar	Palatal	Palato alveolar	Velar	Glottal
Plosive	p b		t d			k g	
Fricative		f v	s -				
						- y	h -

	Bilabial	Labiodental	Alveolar	Palatal	Palato alveolar	Velar	Glottal
Affricate					tc		
					dz		
Nasal	-		-	-		-	
	m		n	ṅ		ṅ	
Lateral			-				
			l				
Approxi-	-			-			
mant	w			j			

Of the 20, /t, k, g, tc, dz n/ can be labialized to obtain [tw, kw, gw tcw dzw nw] which we presently consider as consonant clusters rather than consonants in their own right (as we held before in earlier publications).

Similarly, we consider the secondary articulations [kp, gb] in words such as 'kped' (a heap of, to chew) and 'gbwi' (obvious affirmation) as allophonic variants of the clusters [kw] and [gw], as in 'kwed' (a heap of, to chew) and 'gwi' (obvious affirmation), respectively.

It can safely be concluded from the data in the table above on the inventory and distribution of Mungaka consonants as follows:

i. That all Mungaka consonants occur at initial positions in words.

ii. That only one consonant, /h/, resists the medial position (except in the single word quoted, i.e., "han(g)" which is in itself an onomatopoeic word) while 14 others resist the final position.

iii. That in the same vein (as in (ii) above), only six of the consonants, i.e., /b, d, g, m, n, n/, respectively, occupy all three environments in Mungaka words.

N.B.: Emphasis is on native words, because some of the consonants, such as /k, s/, etc., may occur in some foreign loan words, e.g. finik, (small coin of very low value), druck (to run off or print copies of a book) and katakis (catechist), respectively (also katakisi), etc.

iv. That many Mungaka words are monosyllabic. We shall return to this issue subsequently.

Vowels

Mungaka possesses a system of 9 short (lax) vowels. In actual speech, all 9 vowels can be lengthened by a speaker. However, such length plays no phonemic role. For instance, the Mungaka words tu, mun, vu and bam, etc., (head, person, death, and bag) respectively, can be uttered with or without length in the vowels, and the meanings are not in any way affected. This holds good for all Mungaka words. Diphthongs or vowel glides do not occur in Mungaka, except occasionally in English loans such as pia (pear), bia (beer), etc. Vowel length is therefore non-phonemic in Mungaka.

Glottalized Vowels

Of the 9 vowels in Mungaka, 8 can occur with a glottal stop. The only exception is /o/. Ndangam and Nti have earlier referred to these as truncated vowels, probably on the basis of the consideration that this class of glottalised vowels contrast with their non-glottalised counterparts, as in ba (father) and ba' (to weave) or ti (decorate) and ti' (to meet), etc. We now prefer to consider the glottal stop rightly, as a consonant, but as one that occurs with some vowels in Mungaka, and so, tends to be assimilated by the vowel element of a syllable. This is why we refer to those vowels which occur with the glottal stop as glottalised vowels.

A truncated or glottalised vowel is one which begins with a vowel quality of one kind or another but ends with a narrowing of the glottis, resulting in a consonant quality.

The following is a list of all the vowels and their distribution in Mungaka words:

Table 5.3. Short Non-Truncated Vowels

	Vowel	Initial Position	Medial Position	Final Position
1	/i/	iba (two)	gib (doubt)	ti (to pain)
2	/e/	—	bed (to refuse)	kwe (to return)
3	/ɛ/	—	bɛd (war)	sɛ (also)
4	/a/	a (it...)	tab (shoes)	fa (give)
5	/ɔ/	—	Kɔd (touch)	bo (these)
6	/o/	—	ton (hot)	bo (hand)
7	/o̤/	—	ko̤n (bone)	fo̤ (cold)
8	/u/	u (you)	kun (bed)	ku (to die)
9	/ṳ/	—	bwṳn (breast)	tṳ (tree)

Table 5.4. Truncated and Glottalized Vowels

Sound	Initial Position	Medial Position	Final Position
/i'/	—	fi'ti (initiate)	Fi' (to seize)
/e'/	—	me'ti (to finish)	ke' (to open)
/ɛ'/	—	mɛ'mɛ' (altogether)	mɛ' (all)
/a'/	—	ba'ti (half, part)	fa' (work)
/ɔ'/	—	Kɔ'tań (ladder)	Bɔ' (fear)
/o̤'/	—	Fo̤'ti (to blow)	ko̤' (cough)

Sound	Initial Position	Medial Position	Final Position
/u'/	–	bu'ti (to rule, govern)	bu' (parcel, bundle)
/ṳ'/	–	tṳ'ti (to advise)	ntṳ' (advise)

As with consonants, it can safely be concluded that generally Mungaka vowels resist the initial position in words. They occur mostly in medial and final positions. This observation makes the syllable structure in Mungaka worthy of attention.

Word Lengths in Mungaka

It has earlier been asserted that many Mungaka words are monosyllabic. Although our data in the tables above on both consonants and vowels is a pointer to this conclusion, it must be argued that our conclusion is not drawn wholly from the limited data in this study. Rather, we conclude from both our intuition based on our knowledge of the language, as well as our analysis of exhaustive and elaborate written texts from both religious and secular sources (Biblical texts, dissertations, newsletters i.e., Bo sa' ko e? etc.). It can be estimated that the ratio of monosyllabic to disyllabic and polysyllabic words together is about 3 to 1 if not a little higher.

The Mungaka Word Structure

The word structure in Mungaka varies as follows:

Table 5.5. The Mungaka Word Structure

Structure			Examples
C	n	/n/	(yes)
V	i	/i/	(he, it)
CV	fa	/fa/	(give)

Structure			Examples
CCV	bam	/bam/	(bag)
	mfa	/mfa/	(beads)
	ndi	/ndi/	(ndi)
	nga	/nga/	(that..)
	mba	/mba/	(mad person)
	mpa	/mpa/	(a species of vegetable)
CCVA	mbin	/mbin/	(cockroach)
	ndam	/ndam/	(marriage)
	ntan	/ntan/	(market)
	nkan	/nkan/	(monkey)
	ngam	/ngam/	(conversation)
CCCVC	nkwan	/nkwan/	(slave)

The structure can therefore be reduced to the following formulae:

C^3 initial i.e. C^3

and C^1 final (max) i.e., C^1

It is pertinent in this respect to remark that the initial C element in the C^2 cluster is always a nasal as in the following illustrations:

/mp, mb, mf, nd, nk, ng/ respectively, while the initial C^3 -- -cluster is similarly a nasal as well.

The word "mungwi" /mun gwi/ (woman) reveals the structure CVCCCV, where the maximum C element at the medial position is C^3, but in such a case the presence of a nasal is imperative.

The nasal plays a key role in the initial position, even in changing some verbs into nouns. Examples of this type of transformation abound. E.g.

Table 5.6

Verb		Noun	
kad	(to visit)	nkad	(a visit)
lam	(to marry)	ndam	(a marriage)
tu'	(to advise)	ntu'	(an advice)
tsabni	(to insult each other)	ntsabni	(an insult)
fed	(to oppress)	mfed	(an oppressor)

Tone

Mungaka, like Chinese and many African languages, is a tone language. A tone language is one in which tone patterns form part of the structure of words rather than sentences. Tone itself refers to pitch contour, which serves as a distinctive feature in the voice of the speakers. In Mungaka, tone is phonemic and therefore serves a distinctive role within the sound system of the language. Tone serves to mark both lexical and grammatical distinctions in the language.

Tone languages differ in their tonemes, or the particular patterns of tones that are used. Lima (1973:35) points out that Mungaka makes use of a combination of 'register' and 'contour' tone systems, and that the tone in Mungaka is neither entirely of the type described by K.L. Pike as *Level Pitch Register Tone System for Register Tone Languages*, nor of the type which he describes as *Gliding*

Pitch Tone System for Contour languages. Rather, Mungaka makes use of both lexical and contour tones. Ndangam (1972:22) holds the same view when he states: "…There is also a rising tone which means that the language (Mungaka) is a register tone language with contour (glide) overlap."

Essentially, words are distinguished by two basic tonemes. These are:

i. A high level tone (HL) and
ii. A low level tone (LL)

e.g., taŋ (HL) /taŋ/ (arithmetic, to count)
taŋ (LL) /taŋ/ (ceiling, a form of scabies)
ka (HL) /ka/ (to request payment of a debt)
ka (LL) /ka/ (a container for transporting fowls, past tense particle)
ba (HL) /ba/ (father)
ba (LL) /ba/ we (plural)
ta (HL) /ta/(to play, e.g., a ball, to shine, to sew clothes, bag, etc.)
ta (LL) / ta/(an insect, the father of, etc.)
But there are also examples of rising and falling in the pitch (tones), resulting in the following tonemes:

iii. A Low Rise tone (LR)
iv. A High Rise tone (HR)
v. A High Fall tone (HL) occurring in various grammatical distinctions as in tense and aspect.
vi. A Low Fall tone (LF),

e.g., Ka (LR) / ka/ (grandmother)
kǫ̈ŋ (LR) /kǫ̈ŋ/ (to cry)
taŋ (HR) /taŋ/ (to be tough, e.g., skin, cloth)
dzaŋ (HR) /dzaŋ/ (to split, e.g., a bamboo rope or pitch.)

Words constituted of two syllables generally use the level tones, which may be either both high level or low level or a combination of both of these. Examples of these abound.

Table 5.7

dza'ni	(LL + LL)	/dza'ni/	(to yawn, to dry)
dzo̤̣'ti	(LL + LL)	/dzo̤̣'ti/	(a broom)
dzo̤̣'ti	(HL + HL)	/dzo̤̣'ti/	(to lean objects on a wall)
fa'ni	(HL + LL)	/fa'-ni/	(a quarrel)
ta'ti	(HL + LL)	/ ta'-ti /	(a road language or intersection)

We can conclude from our data above that Mungaka can be classified as both a register and tone language, as it employs both level and falling/rising tones.

It is also obvious that Mungaka, being a tone language, differs considerably from both English and French, which are stress-timed and syllable-timed, respectively. However, Mungaka-speakers who are bilingual in French and English will agree that Mungaka is perhaps more akin to the former than the latter, not only on the basis of the well-known and interesting coincidence between the French word bon /bon/ for 'good', and the Mungaka word boŋ /boŋ/ for 'good' as well, but also on close similarities in rhythm, both of which are perceived as isosyllabic, unlike English, which is isochronous (i.e., stressed-timed).

Mungaka: A Written (Codified) Language

Mungaka not only exists in its oral form, but it has also enjoyed and continues to enjoy the rare privilege of a codified language in Cameroon. Today, thanks to the laudable effort of SIL, i.e., Summer

Institute of Linguistics (Société Internationale de Linguistique) in Cameroon, several Cameroon languages (Bafut, Lamnso, etc.) have joined the list of written languages in the North West Province in particular.

The orthography in use, as can be verified from their publications, is slightly different from that in which Mungaka is written. In this way, the Mungaka orthography, side by side with that of Duala, will for a long time to come remain classic and unique in its genre, as many more languages in Cameroon will be written in the modified orthography. If this modified orthography gains popularity, as indeed it is likely to, then future writings in Mungaka will also make use of the new system.

To describe Mungaka as a literary language is, of course, not tantamount to placing it on a par with greater literary languages such as English, French, German, Chinese, Arabic and so on. Firstly, few people can read Mungaka, and even fewer can write it. In fact, fewer than about 5,000 people can be said to be effectively literate in the language, whose domain of literacy is largely restricted to religious literature. As a matter of fact, it was through its written form that Mungaka came to be a lingua franca in the North West Province (the Grassfields region of the former Southern Cameroons, as it was popularly known then).

Early Efforts on the Codification of Mungaka

Mungaka came into writing through the early diligent work of Protestant Missionaries from Basel. Following the arrival of Ferdinand Ernst and Rev. Rudolf Leimbacker in Bali Nyonga on Sunday May 17th 1903, after a prior negotiation between a three-man delegation led by Rev. Eugen Schuler, and the Fon of Bali at that time, His Highness Fonyonga I, a Basel Mission Station (now the Presbyterian Church in Cameroon) was founded. The missionaries immediately settled down to their new and challenging task, with a firm hand 'on the plough'. They were faced with the task of learning

Mungaka, which was considered the sine qua non instrument with which their evangelical mission was to be carried out.

Besides the hospitable character of the natives, it is suggested by Malcolm and Tucker that one deciding factor for the founding of the station in Bali was the linguistic assumption that Mungaka was found to be phonetically less complicated and therefore easier to learn, at least to those foreign missionaries.

By 1905 the effort of those early Missionaries in the codification of Mungaka based on a slightly modified orthography of German was already brought to fruition with pathfinder publications such as a grammar of Mungaka in German (later translated into English) and a Mungaka vocabulary glossary. Shortly afterwards, in 1906, a *Bali Primer* (Fibel) saw the light and was meant to serve as a first manual for the teaching of the language. This primer made great fame, and indeed it was a novelty. It ushered in some innovations: formal language learning (both as mother-tongue and as a foreign language) and literacy. It was the first and the last time that the people of Bali and North Westerners were initiated into formal education by learning an indigenous language, their own language. Generations later were to begin with English before reverting to Mungaka, and today it is a mere anachronism to our youths.

By 1915, a translation of Bible stories was available. It was not until 1933 that the first publication of the New Testament was put into the hands of Christians, a revision of which came much later, in the early 1960s.

It is known that the driving force behind and responsible for the commendable achievement in the realm of publications was Adolf Vielhauer, whose protracted stay in Bali earned him real proficiency in almost all skills in Mungaka. Of course, invaluable credit is also due to Rev. Elisa Ndifon (Gwansalla) whose brief stay in Germany on the invitation of the Missionaries in Basel was equally instrumental in the revision of some of the publications, particularly the new edition of the Holy Bible as well as the Hymn

Book– *Ntsi Nikob bi Ndzobdzob ni tsu Mungaka.* But the preponderant role which Fonyonga I and Galega II each played indirectly in the fulfilment of this task is such that deserves special mention in this chapter. For a list of some of the religious publications in Mungaka alluded to or discussed above, see our bibliography.

Figure 5.1. Rev. Pastor Elisa Ndifon, Editor-in-chief of the Mungaka version of the Holy Bible. Knighted Gwansalla and admitted into the Nkomship by V.S. Galega II in recognition of his outstanding leadership in the Christian faith.

Secular Publications in Mungaka

Apart from the many religious literary publications mentioned above, it would be true to assert that in North West Province in general, and in Bali in particular, written Mungaka has in the main, remained the domain of private writing, such as in private letters among relatively few who were schooled in it. This is particularly the case with letters and documents meant to remain cryptic—personal wills, for instance. Of special mention in this category are sermons that are meant to be read out on pulpits in some Presbyterian Churches, although the practice is greatly on the decline.

To the above should be added the case of desperate attempts that have been made, though in the distant past, to preserve Mungaka in secular documentation. Two examples deserve special mention here.

The first is a popular newsletter entitled '**Bo Sa' Ko e**' (What is the news?) which appeared in the sixties, the editor of which was Ndangam Augustine. It carried exciting articles on the history and cultural aspects of Bali Chamba and Bali Nyonga people and was greatly appreciated, especially among the Bali kith and kin for its traditional and innovative writings. It finally died a natural death, and in spite of repeated calls for its revival by the elite, it has remained in oblivion. The question, notwithstanding, is to know how many people would be willing to read it if it were revived. Besides, today's elites appear to have many more reading options than in the past and who doubts that the reappearance of such a local paper may even be opprobrious to some people.

The second is a courageous and laudable attempt at producing a Mungaka dictionary, the lexicographer of whom is another devoted veteran Swiss Missionary lady whose protracted stay in the North West Province earned her the honorific appellation. Na (Mother), resulting in her full name Na Weber. The laudable project, which she single-handedly engaged in, has, to the best of our knowledge, not seen the light of day yet. However, unpublished sections of it, which we have had the privilege of seeing, reveal that if the project were achieved, it would undoubtedly be a historical monument that would add yet another contribution to the once-prolific character of documentation in Mungaka.

Anglicised Orthography of Mungaka

There has arisen among some educated Bali people, but who unfortunately cannot read and write Mungaka an ambition to encode in the Mungaka script. Unable, therefore, to use the Mungaka orthography properly, they have tended to be as eclectic as possible in adapting an anglicised orthography which nevertheless results in an unorthodox but fairly intelligible script. Examples of orthographical representation of such script include:

Table 5.8

Typical Mungaka Orthography	Anglicised Orthography	Meaning
baṅ	bang	walking stick
taṅ	tang	arithmetic, to count
ɣan	ghan	a thief
tsaṅ	chang	chains
fa'	Fah	work

Proper Names in Mungaka Orthography

Today, few proper names of people and place names have retained their original Mungaka pronunciations. The reason is obvious: their spellings are either anglicised or frenchified, a phenomenon that is unfortunately true of nearly all African names. Such mutilation in the spellings of personal and place names, as found on maps, equally results in phonemic distortions. This explains why, when certain names in Cameroon are read out on the radio, in classrooms or in meetings, it is sometimes hardly possible to recognize them as such. This is particularly the case in English (perhaps more than other European languages) because of the wide disparity that exists between speech and writing in English, the two hardly ever being in a one-to-one correspondence, as is practically the case in Spanish, for instance. A few personal and place names in Bali will illustrate the point and thus minimize the likelihood of the point being belaboured:

Table 5.9

Mungaka Version	Phonetic Representation	English Version
Mo'iwo̤	[mɔ'iwo̤]	Mohiwo, Moiwo
Lo̤ga	[ləga]	Loga, Lega
Kṳnu	[kṳnu]	Kunu, Kinu
Bṳṅa	[bṳṅa]	Bunga
Mṳtsa'	[mṳtsa']	Muchah, Micha
Ndzenka'	[ndzenka']	Ndzenka, Njenka

The fact that today several English spelling variants of the same names exist, as the table above illustrates, reveals to what extent an orthographic solution can alienate the representation of a phonemic system. While we do not here insinuate that the best way to obviate the inherent linguistic danger alluded to above is to revert to the Mungaka orthography in its entirety, (far from it) we nevertheless draw attention to the anglicisation of vernacular names which in itself is a practical solution, but which, on the other hand has in the process modified and thus de-acculturalized our folk names, rendering them neither Mungaka nor English. After all, is this not the unfortunate fate of every educated African, that in the quest for education, he has half lost his original cultural identity?

The Mungaka Orthography

Mungaka is written on the basis of the alphabetic system. The following is a list of consonant and vowel letters, as well as punctuation marks used.

Literacy in Mungaka

The Alphabet

Aa Bb Cc Dd Ee Ff Gg Hh Ii Jj Kk Ll Mn Nn Oo Pp Qq Rr Ss Tt Uu Vv Ww Xx Yy Zz

Consonant Letters:

Bb Dd Ff Gg Hh Dz dz Kk Li Mm Nn Ńń Ṅṅ, Pp Kw Rr Ss Tt Vv Ww Zz ɤ

Vowel Letters

A	a	a̤	ā	a’
E	e	ē	e’	
I	i	ī	i’	
O	o	o’		
O̱	o̱	o̱’		

O̤ o̤ o̤’
U u u’
Ṳ ṳ u̯ u̯’

Punctuation

. , ; : . .. ? “ ” ( ) -

Figures: 1 2 3 4 5 6 7 8 9 10 ....

LANGUAGE USAGE: SPOKEN MUNGAKA

The spoken medium in Mungaka varies to a greater or lesser extent, as the case may be, from the more formal written medium. While the written form is formal and standardized, the spoken medium is less formal, more diversified, and characterised by phenomena such as code-switching and/or mixing and various forms of linguistic interference.

Language purity and interference

There are still in Bali today a few native speakers of Mungaka who can by dint of the purity of their speech be described as language ‘purists’. These are people who consciously or inadvertently speak and or write in ‘pure’ and unadulterated Mungaka. Those who do so consciously, deliberately endeavour to eschew all forms of interference, be they phonological, lexical or grammatical. In practical terms, this implies that this class of speakers seeks to avoid the influence of other languages with which Mungaka has come into contact such as English, Pidgin-English and French, as well as any of the scores of other indigenous Cameroon languages. But it actually requires great effort to achieve such an ideal at a time when education, travel, mass media, urbanisation, and other similar factors militate in favour of various forms of code mixing in use as Bali, henceforth, ceases to be an island. The predominant influence of English in particular on Mungaka corroborates the view that the purist attitude of the few who belong to this school of thought is doomed to failure.

Mungaka and English

While it is worthwhile to laud the efforts of these apparent purists, who are jealously guarding the purity of the language (but not other aspects of our ever-changing culture), on the claim that a good bilingual is one who succeeds to separate different codes, and uses one language at a time, it is equally vital to accept the truism that one direction towards which a language develops is the acquisition of loan words amongst others. Also, linguistic interference is an inevitable feature of usage among bilinguals and polyglots, and can consequently hardly be controlled, let alone legislated against.

Today, there are many English loans in Mungaka that many native speakers, not excluding some of the so-called purists, would readily take some of these words for native Mungaka words, probably because their pronunciations have been smoothly adapted into the Mungaka sound system. Examples which abound include:

Table 5.10

English	Mungaka
coat	/kuti/
hospital	/wasipita/
tax	/taksi/
blanket	/plankṳtu/
pound (sterling)	/pon/
pastor	/pasito/ etc,

Syllabification is more commonly used.

While the younger generation prefers the standard English pronunciations of these words while speaking Mungaka, the older generation tends to use the Mungaka pronunciations above. In either case, it is the English form of the words that is used. The reason is obvious: namely, that they deal with foreign or imported concepts, and so the borrowed forms of the words are more expressive and effective than native coinages or the descriptive devices that exist for some of them.

Mungaka and other Languages

As already mentioned, the Bali Nyonga are very eclectic. Mungaka has therefore borrowed from other languages. As a result of early trade with some tribes in Cameroon and Nigeria, Mungaka came to borrow from the Ejagham and the Bayangi in Manyu Division and the Efik in Nigeria. Although these foreign languages are not widely spoken in Bali, they are quite popular in the domain of cultural singing and dancing of the well-known Nyangkwe dance. This particular cultural dance is one of the many popular dances executed in cultural forums such as at funeral ceremonies and other cultural manifestations. It is often interesting to watch the Nyangkwe display, especially on New Year's Day at the Fon's open piazza, as it has become customary for it to be organised on every first of January. What is interesting about it is that it is one of the few cultural dances that are sung entirely in a foreign language other than Mubako. And those who are eloquent in it are greatly admired. Bali people who are bilingual in Mungaka and another Cameroon language take delight in showing off their versatility because from the point of view of Bali philosophy, this is of a great boon in both military and diplomatic matters. Those who cannot afford knowledge of another language swing to the other end of the pendulum and become rather loyal and chauvinistic to Mungaka. On the other hand, most Bali people have the weakness of assuming that other people, viz., non-Balians, understand Mungaka. In fact, many of them would be taken aback if they came across a North Westerner who neither understood nor spoke Mungaka —as if Mungaka were a universal language. Even English, the most widely spoken language in standard) does not claim to be universal.

Mungaka and Traditional Singing

As far as traditional or cultural singing is concerned, it would be truer today to assert that with the exception of classical songs connected with traditional religious festivities such as Lela, Danga and Voma, sung in Mubako, (See Titanji, Chapter Four) as well as dirges and war songs (epics), traditional, pop and other light-hearted songs now tend to be sung sometimes in a combination of Mungaka and Pidgin-English or other local languages. This is so because of the accessibility of Pidgin English to all and sundry. Besides, it now seems fashionable amongst the youths to sing in English for a change (a reflexion of their speaking habits), and the language variety readily accessible and vulgar enough for the purpose is Pidgin English.

The popular Nda-lung (harp) Association of Youths, a cultural group in Bali and other urban centres in Cameroon, is known to have made, and continues to make a name for itself with several local pop song compositions in which Pidgin English blends distinctly with Mungaka. And this is an innovation in Bali Culture. Pointed examples of these include the lines:

> Yo bo wonderful e. wonder wonder wonderful e
> One day one day me too a go die e
> Nku ba, nku ba mu nkab ni mbo ma
> You bi ma woman e, ma woman, e, etc.

Such a phenomenon clearly illustrates the extent to which Mungaka is beginning to interrelate with other languages. And this too is language growth and development, although it must be argued that whether this is a favourable or unfavourable development of the language is quite another question —one of value judgement.

NAMES AND NAMING IN BALI

To the riddle, "What is it that every individual owns, but nearly never makes use of except other people?" The obvious answer is a *name*.

A name is very important because it identifies every individual and distinguishes him/her from all other people in the community. But it also conveys information about one's place of origin; that is, nationality, country, clan and sometimes, village or even family in at least a majority of cases. This is why we are often able to say off-hand at the mention of a name whether the bearer is of Japanese, Chinese, English, French or African origin, broadly speaking. Similarly, it is generally easy at the national level for people to pinpoint a person's clan or village of origin from the name he or she bears, although it must be pointed out that this phenomenon is gradually dying out. Notwithstanding the fair probability of coincidences of identical names from different countries, let alone different tribes within the same country, it is arguably true that today, for instance, it is common experience, in Africa in general and Cameroon in particular, to find people who bear or give names (to their children) that are foreign to their clans or villages. They might simply have opted for a name of a renowned personality: politician, successful businessman, doctor, etc., irrespective of the ethnological origin of the name. They may even have simply been attracted by the 'beauty' of a name. While such a practice, carried out advertently or inadvertently, may well be a proper step in the direction of our, so-much solicited national unity as part of our doctrine of Communal Liberalism today, it remains however to be observed that the maxim "Tell me your name, and I will tell you where you come from," is still a verifiable reality in Cameroon. It goes without saying that our definition of 'name' here excludes the so-called Christian name (Prénom) for obvious reasons. The identification and matching of names to corresponding clans and villages, and consequently, cultures, is, in fact, to a certain extent, a clue to the recognition of the sound systems of the different languages, as well as language and cultural affinity. English names sound English, in much the same way as Mungaka names sound Mungaka; thus, Bali-Nyonga names may be (and are) identical with Bali-Kumbat or Bali-Gashu names on the grounds of cultural and/or historical affinity.

Philosophy of Naming in Bali

In Bali, the name a person bears can be seen as an index of information about the individual himself, his family or the whole tribe at large. A name may be associated with, or related to, a past event in the family, a family wish or problem, an apprehension, a premonition, a belief, an aspiration, a reminiscence, names of household objects and so on. For this reason, every name in Bali has a situational meaning—indeed, a deep-seated and well-intentioned meaning. Thus, when a name is mentioned or called out, intelligible or initiated listeners can easily associate it with a specific event in time, e.g., they can infer that the bearer of the name was born, for instance, during wartime, a period of peace, abundance or famine, or during a particular cultural event such as Lela, Voma, etc. A name may also suggest to the bearer whether the person bearing the name comes from a family of many children or one that has lost many other children. Similarly, it may provide an immediate clue as to whether the bearer is a twin child—female or male or one that was born immediately following twins. Some names convey information as to the social status of the persons concerned, while some can even be said to be reminiscent of the specific day of the week on which the individual was born. A name is therefore not simply given at random, but carefully thought out to portray something considered important to the family.

Categories of Names and Naming in Bali

There are different categories of names in Bali, and the same individual may well bear several different names corresponding to different categories. There are principally, amongst others, the following: Birth names, Title Names, Marriage or Wedding Names and Parent Names.

Birth Names

In Bali, a newly born baby acquires a surname usually known as *lun-nkaŋ* (literally, a corn beer name) given in a naming ceremony exactly one week after birth. The ceremony is attended by close members of the family. Corn beer, a locally brewed drink which is an important traditional drink, is served at the occasion. At the salient moment of the naming, an elderly member of the family who performs the ceremony, dips his/her finger into a cup of the corn-beer and places it on the baby's tongue while pronouncing the name for the first time in the hearing of all the attendees. The young baby who hitherto was referred to simply as "mon" (baby), now bears a name. The significance of the name is then made known to all present. This is usually followed by feasting.

Linguistic Sources of Names

There are primarily two linguistic sources of names. These are Mubako and Mungaka, respectively, in that order of frequency. Although Mubako is not widely used in Bali today as a spoken language, it is nevertheless reserved for specific salient domains, such as for names and naming, classical singing, as in the case of Lela, Danga and Voma, respectively and the pouring of libations during traditional religious ceremonies, especially at the Lela and Voma shrines.

Frequency Order of Names

It has already been mentioned that some Bali names are of Mubako origin, while others are of Mungaka origin. This means that they are derived from the Mubako lexeme and the Mungaka lexeme, respectively—a variation that has obvious linguistic repercussions.

Mubako and Mungaka Birth Names

It can be assessed that about 70% of Bali indigenes bear Mubako names. The consequence is that many people bear names whose meanings they do not know unless they actually make an effort to find out from a Mubako-speaking person what they mean. And there are many people who are eager to know the meanings of their names.

In this respect, Nwana and Ndangam, in an effort to acquaint inquisitive youths today with the meanings of their Mubako names, published a pamphlet (1981) that attempts to give the English interpretations of 79 male and 98 female names. Of the total of 177 names they studied, 137 are Mubako, while the rest of the 40 are Mungaka names. We think that the approximate ratio of 3:1, that is, 77.40% to 22.59% taken at random, illustrates the approximate ratio of Mubako to Mungaka names in Bali today.

Recently, Fokwang (1986) has published a more ambitious brochure containing a glossary of 660 Mubako and Mungaka names with their English interpretations in an attempt to familiarise people with the meanings of the names they may want to select for their children. The names are classified according to Mubako and Mungaka types, male and female or unisex types respectively, with their meanings in English. About 69.10% (456) of the names are Mubako, while the remaining 30.90% (204 names) are of Mungaka origin. Although a more exhaustive study based on a larger corpus of names may reveal a variation from the present percentages, we remain persuaded that there are by far more Mubako names than Mungaka names. It can safely be concluded from this that, although

Mubako is today a near-defunct language in Bali, it is still alive in the area of names and naming.

Notwithstanding their statistical rarity, some people prefer Mungaka to Mubako names, probably because of the double advantage which the phenomenon offers. Firstly, it has a self-explanatory meaning to the Mungaka-speaking folk and therefore does not require any more than perhaps a deep-structural meaning as the surface-structural (literal) meaning is often obvious, e.g., Ndibmun = one's own time. (There is time for everything). Secondly, it gives room for creativity and originality. A speaker of the language can well coin a name to suit a particular purpose or situation, whereas with a Mubako name, one must always select from an existing list of names, e.g., Ganse, Buma, Sema, Sigala, Yeba, etc. Of course, a Mubako name, too, some may argue, has an advantage over a Mungaka name: that of 'mystification' since the significance of the name remains obscure to all except Mubako-speakers. Furthermore, it is felt by many that a Mubako name serves as an umbilical cord linking the present to the past, the Bali-Nyonga to the Bali-Chamba and therefore, Mungaka to Mubako. In this way, it reminds every Bali person of their historical origin.

Weekday Names

One common source of a name in Bali is to draw directly from the names of the days of the traditional eight-day week. According to this practice, a newly born baby is simply given a name, the name of the day on which it is born depending on its sex, since the names of some weekdays are specifically assigned to the male sex (majority) and some (a few) to the female sex. The names of the days of the week in Bali are in Mungaka, and so these names are naturally Mungaka names. The following are the weekdays:

Table 5.11

Name of Day of the Week	Weekday Birth Name and Sex
Ngo̱' (Ngoh)	Ngo' (Ngoh) (Male)
	Fongo' (Fongoh) M
	Ndango' (Ndangoh) M
Ndansi	Ndansi (M)
Nko̱'ntan (Nkohntan)	Nko'ntan (Nkohntan) (Female)
Ntan, Ntanba'ni	Mantan, Ninantan (F)
Foncham	Foncham (M)
Ntungwen, Ntungwen	Ntungwen, Ntungwen (M)
	Fongwen (M)
Ntanmbutu	Fombutu (M)
Dzimbufuṅ, Dzimbufung	Fofuŋ, Fofung (M)

Note
M = Male Name
F = Female Name

As can be seen from the table above, the first six weekdays are retained in their entirety as birth names, while the last two are slightly modified to undergo minor morphological alterations. 'Ntan' in the first case denotes 'market' while 'Dzi…' in the second case implies 'a holiday.' Both have simply been replaced by another common prefix, Fo..., which literally means 'the Chief or Fon of.' Except in these two cases where 'Fo' occurs as a prefix in both names, 'Fo' occurring in many names denotes a social status, namely, that of a titleholder. Examples of personalities in Bali who, for historical reasons, bear such title names (sub-chiefs) include, amongst others: Fotikali, Fokundom (Fokindem), Foset, Fowon, etc. Malcolm Green (1982:41) misses the point when he refers to a personality in Bali as "Ba for German" when he should actually say Ba Fo German. We shall presently examine the question of the titleholder category of names.

Title Names

The second category of names is what may be referred to as 'Title Names'. These names are usually borne by dignitaries on whom traditional honorific titles have been conferred. According to Bali tradition, such titles, in many cases, are hereditary and are usually handed down from father to son. In this case, a son who inherits his father's title endeavours to live up to the name in order to eschew the probability of such a title being withdrawn from him and his entire family. What opprobrium!

Types of Title Names

There are principally two types of title names. These are

a. those that are acquired at birth, and
b. those that are conferred by virtue of traditional functions assigned to the title holders.

Although it is possible to establish a strict hierarchical taxonomy of the various titles, such a task is beyond the purpose of this study.

Title Names Acquired at Birth

In Bali, adult male princes (bonfon) are referred to as 'Tita'. This honorific title is affixed at the beginning of the personal name of every adult prince and serves to distinguish princes from ordinary people, not necessarily so much as a feature of social discrimination as a mark of identification of members of the royal family. Thus, a prince whose birth name is Lesiga, for instance, is referred to as Tita Lesiga. It is interesting and pertinent to note that in many cases, users tend to delete the personal names of the addressees, retaining, thereby, in the process, only the title, Tita for short. This results in an impersonal form of address. It has, however, been observed that there is a tendency amongst many Bali folk today to extrapolate on the use of 'Tita' as pet names. Thus, during conversation, the titles 'Tita' and 'Mfon' respectively are used in the place of an individual's personal names as a symbol of intimacy. They may also be used in situations where the speakers do not know the actual names of the addressees. These are, however, mere euphemisms of names that refer to males.

Title Names Conferred

Title names that are conferred by virtue of traditional functions assigned to the title holders are many and varied according to existing functions within the traditional structure. These include the following among others: Tutuwan, Gwe, Nwana, Sama, Tita and Komfon. Fokwang (1986:10-12) has attempted definitions of these titles which we consider adequate for his purpose and ours.

Tutuwan

This title is given to a flag bearer or one who carries traditional insignia during yearly ceremonies, such as the Lela festival or other important events.

It is significant to point out that the title 'Tutuwan' has been personalised by some of these title holders who have come to be known as 'Tutuwan' almost to the exclusion of their personal birth names. This, in a way, portrays the extent to which public life can influence private life, at least in Bali.

Gwe

A title name given to traditional scouts who guard the Bali flags and play the role of jesters or comedians while maintaining order during public festivities. As Fokwang (1986:12) points out, the name has come to serve as a prefix to their personal names, often affixed to their birth names, hence, Gwe Pamuga, etc.

Nwana

Although this is a birth name often given to a male child born in the month of the year during which a traditional cult known as Voma is performed, it is above all a title name conferred as a mark of distinction for public services on people who henceforth become dignitaries of the Bali state cult known as Voma. The word 'Nwana' is of Mubako origin and denotes a guard, the rain or a spirit.

Sama

Sama is also an ambiguous name because it serves as both a birth name and a title name. Firstly, it is the birth name that is automatically given to a male twin. Where there are two male twin children involved, one is called Samgwa'a and the other Samjela. (Nagwa and Najela, respectively, for twin girls). As a title, it is a name conferred on a man who, having undergone a special initiation, officiates in the cult activities associated with the Lela festival. As in the case of Nwana, it is not often easy to distinguish between a Mr. Sama and a Sama. In the context of Lela, the expression Ba Sama (ba plural morpheme) refers unequivocally to the title holders. The word "Sama" is also a Mubako expression for "prince." Thus, the Sama were originally princes; only later were "commoners", i.e., ordinary people, or non-members of the royal family, included in the group.

Tita

Tita means prince, master, captain, or leader.

Komfon (Gwan)

The 'Komfon' are traditional councillors. They occupy a prestigious place within the hierarchy of title holders in Bali. They are the most numerous among title holders (conferred). The title of nkom (sing) Kom (pl.) is often conferred by the Fon on deserving appointees, usually men only, as a symbol of honour in appreciation of their special devotion or contribution to the cultural heritage of the kingdom. According to this tradition, a new name in Mubako is carefully selected to reflect the recipient's special character, merit, speciality, philosophy, or even the political climate at the time, and is assigned to him. A general title name to all who belong to this category is Gwan, which serves as a prefix to the full name. Thus, the newly assigned name is affixed to the prefix Gwan. Care is taken to ensure that the name is never duplicated for any other person. Thus, there is usually only one such title name in the whole of Bali. In this way, there can never be any confusion as to the identity of a particular Nkom.

It is estimated that there are about 58 Komfon today. The following are a few of the Komfon on names that have been selected at random for illustration.

Table 5.11

Name	Literal Meaning	Literary Meaning
1. Gwan-Kudvalla	one who handles the corpse	He who takes care of the dead.
2. Gwan-pefok	who paves the way to the bush	The pathfinder. He who settles first in a yet-to-develop area.
3. Gwan-mesia	one who brings dew/water	He who brings life to the village.

Name	Literal Meaning	Literary Meaning
4. Gwan-lima	burden	He who bears the burden (for others).
5. Gwan-dua	the old	The old man of the clan (symbol of wisdom, the mentor)
6. Gwan-kobe	Looks after new arrivals	The one who is in charge of publicising the newly appointed- the announcer.
7. Gwan-gwa'a	The big	The symbol of greatness (leader).
8. Gwan-nyama	Which shines	The one who brings light (enlightener).
9. Gwan-nua	The eye	The one who sees for others – the mentor; the Fon's eyes.
10. Gwan-fogbe	Who lives in the bush	He who lives in a yet-to-be developed area.

NB: Each name is imbued with some patriotic characteristic, and the bearer is consequently expected to live up to it.

Mutual Exclusion

It follows that dignitaries who bear title names have a choice between using their birth names and their newly acquired title names. More often than not, the use of one name, at least officially, excludes the use of the other, although in a few cases some Komfon combine both birth names and title name, resulting in compound names.

It has, however, been observed that a great majority of the Komfon are officially and popularly known by their title names.

These dignitaries have either relegated their birth names to secondary positions or have almost entirely given up their names. In the majority of cases where the title name is propagated and used almost to the exclusion of the birth name, such a name consequently becomes the family name and is borne by all the offspring of the family. This explains why the names Gwan-pefok, Gwan-mesia, Gwan-lima, Gwan-dua, Gwan-kobe, Gwangwa'a, Gwan-nyama, and Gwan-fogbe, amongst others, are not borne exclusively by the title holders (original or successors), but also by all members of the respective families in each case. The argument for this is not far-fetched: a family name is the greatest overt symbol that all members of the same family should share in common, generation after generation, and being in itself a status symbol, it no doubt serves as the identification mark of the family. After all, the daughter or the son of a 'Gwan', or Nkom, is immediately identified and respected as the daughter or son of a noble. And Bali culture clearly attaches great importance to this 'MoNkom' phenomenon.

In spite of the dominant practice, it has somehow become highly debatable amongst the younger generation as to whether title holders of this category (Nkom), and even the others, ought to be encouraged to relegate, neglect or drop their birth names in favour of title names as official names. In the same vein, some extremists even question why children are allowed to bear titles borne by their fathers instead of bearing their fathers' birth names. The controversies arise from the closely related arguments that, in the first place, a title name is not altogether permanent. It is temporary in the sense that it can be withdrawn as mentioned earlier, in the event of a misdeed or gross misbehaviour on the part of the titular holder of the title. If, therefore, this ignominious situation were to arise, and the name had to be withdrawn, what would happen to the scores of people who already bear the name officially, verbally and even in official documents? Problematic. Secondly, do children have a right to bear title names, and thereby share in the honour that goes along with each title, when in reality, they have not achieved any particular feat to deserve the title? The exponents of this view argue by analogy that the children of Honourable Members of Parliament (MPs) cannot be addressed as 'Honourable', nor can the son of a Lord in Britain be addressed as 'Lord' while his father is still alive. However, such analogies can in no way validate the argument, particularly as they make reference to cultural realities outside of Bali Nyonga culture. The Bali culture must be seen and judged in its own right, in spite of its dynamic characteristics.

The status quo in this respect remains what it is, namely, that the great majority of the Komfon have opted to use the 'Gwan -- form of their names, although there are nevertheless cases of families of the Komfon category who have opted to use the birth names of their family head rather than the 'Gwan' form of their title names, The members of the Lima family, in this respect, are hardly known and addressed as Gwankudvalla. The title name is uniquely held and borne by the family head, who is usually addressed by this title almost exclusively in traditional circles. Gwannua and Gwan-Kudla, who were recently raised to the title of 'Komfon', have so far retained their family birth names as official names. They remain Messrs Ndangam and Tata, respectively. Their title names only feature in traditional circles, mostly. It must be pointed out that so far, the question as to which of the two types of names a person should use officially remains the prerogative of the individual. The problem of option only arises today because of the duality of roles played by these dignitaries in society. In former times, accession to the title automatically resulted in the use of the title name at all times and for all intents and purposes. But times are changing, and so is custom, too.

Marriage Names

The next category of names that we present in this study is what we prefer to refer to as *Marriage Names*, from a literal translation of the Mungaka expression Luŋ ndam, i.e. Name Marriage.

It is customary in Bali Nyonga to give every bride a pet name on the occasion of her wedding. The name, which is often carefully selected to symbolise a specific virtue, the incarnation of which the newly married woman is supposed to be, is chosen by the bride's family-in-law.

There are in Bali today, many married women whose marriage names have completely overshadowed and/or submerged their birth names. Of course, the success of this depends largely on the interest which husbands take in constantly addressing their wives by their new names. Such a pet name obviously has a love connotation. Thus, every housewife who is addressed by her marriage name immediately feels flattered and cajoled. In some cases, marriage names are actually promoted by housewives themselves, who prefer to be called by such pet names rather than by their original names.

From the cultural and psychological points of view, a marriage name is extremely important not only to the couple but also, especially, to society at large. It is a symbol and a constant reminder to the woman that henceforth, she has acquired a new status in life. In the same vein, it assures all the other onlookers in the society, both interested and uninterested parties alike, that the young woman in question is no longer the 'free' individual with a wide latitude of liberty that she was before. She is now under someone's eyes and protection. She is now someone's 'bag' (to use a Mungaka expression) into which her husband will henceforth store his valuables.

Table 5.13 lists some common marriage names and their meanings.

Table 5.13. Common Marriage Names

Name in Mubako	Literal Meaning	Literary Meaning
1. Vadkilla	My death bed	She is my death-mate. Only death will do us (husband and wife) part.
2. Weteba	Cold water	The source of life to the man and the woman who will henceforth regulate the man's temperament.
3. Bisona	It is good	The symbol of a happy home.
4. Sobila	The moon is up	She is a light to the man's feet. She is also as lovely as the moon and will shine as the moon.
5. Nyongtema	Heart of the matter	She will bring meaning to the home.
6. Kehtema	Open the heart	She will penetrate her husband's heart, and so will he. She is a well-beloved partner.
7. Petema	Open the mind	She will make her husband more reasonable in life.
8. Sadmia	Suitable	She befits her husband. Both are well-matched.
9. Nahyella	Fair complexion	She will shine in manners as in body.

Name in Mubako	Literal Meaning	Literary Meaning
10. Ntsimfoni	Cold water	Cold water (as above) and all that it means to man as opposed to hot water that is dangerous. Henceforth, her husband will have cold water to quench his thirst.
11. Nahsala	Suits me	She befits me, i.e., she is exactly what I (husband) look for in a wife. My dream has come true.

To the above list, also included are the following: Nahkula Nahbula, Nahkum, Nahdinga, Sanyonga, etc., amongst others.

Mother-Child Names, Father-Child Names

Another equally interesting category of names is mother-child names and father-child names, respectively.

When a woman gives birth to her first child, she acquires a new name, which we have described as a 'mother-child' name. The woman is then named after the child. The linguistic process of the naming consists of appending the morpheme 'Ma', i.e. 'Mother of', to the child's name. For instance, if the child is named Babila, her mother automatically becomes Ma-Babila, literally meaning 'the mother of Babila'. Later on in life, she may have many other children, but she retains the original name, and this poses no embarrassment whatsoever to the other children, in whose minds no doubt is cast as to whether they, too, like Babila, are not the legitimate children of their mother. Although statistically speaking, most women who bear names of this type are named after their first issue, there are nevertheless women who are named after children born to them later in life. The reasons for this vary, amongst which is the factor that at the time a woman has her first baby, she is perhaps still too intimately attached to her marriage name to drop it in preference to a mother-child name.

It is worth pointing out that, inasmuch as there is the phenomenon of mother-child name, there is understandably also that of father-child name. A father may also be named after his son or daughter. In this case, the morpheme 'Ta', i.e., 'father-of', is equally appended to the child's name. Thus, Ta-Babila is the father of Babila. For obvious reasons, the practice is more prevalent among mothers than fathers, who tend to have a lesser attachment to their children than their ever-present mothers. Besides, the men aspire to other distinguished title names. In all cases, however, the father of twin children is automatically called Tanyi while their mother is referred to as Manyi. (Incidentally, the two names Tanyi and Manyi are widely used among many tribes in the grasslands region to refer to the father and mother of twins) triplets, etc., respectively.

Interestingly enough, it is common to come across women and men who bear such names even after the death of their child. In such a case, the name becomes a mere souvenir symbol. It may remind even the woman who may never have another child, that after all, she has had a child before, in a society that attaches absolute importance to childbirth as a vindication of one's chastity, one's family nobility and one's womanhood.

It may be useful, and even interesting for the purpose of comparison, to allude to an apparently similar practice among the Bassa and other tribes regarding mother-child and father-child names. While the Bassa people, by using the morpheme *Ngo* (meaning 'child of'), name a child after their parents, e.g., Ngo Nguidjol means 'the daughter of Nguidjol', the reverse is the case among the Bali, who name a parent after their child. Such variation not only serves to illustrate Cameroon's rich culture, but also, and especially, the diversity and importance that different communities attach to the principles of names and naming.

The study on names and naming in this chapter has revealed that there are different categories of names and that each category corresponds to specific circumstances and motives. A name is therefore portrayed as symbolic and meaningful within the context of Bali culture.

The significance which names have may further be illustrated by the following Mubako and Mungaka-based names:

Table 5.14. Select Bali Names and their Meanings

Name	Literal Meaning	Literary Meaning
1. Babila	Father is back or father has come back.	Name given to a male child born after the death of his father. It is believed that the child is a reincarnation of his father.
2. Na'bila	Mother is back or Mother has come back	A name given to a female child born after the death of her mother, or a close relative.
3. Bengyela	I have hung up my cutlass	A name given to a child born after a war, or a fight or even a family quarrel. It is the symbol of burying the hatchet.
4. Bidbila	The house has come back to normal	A name given to a child after a family reconciliation.
5. Dayebga	You can't abandon your father's land or the fatherland	A name given as a symbol of patriotism, intended to kindle the spirit of nationalism.
6. Gadinga	The Fon's spear or flag	It is the symbol of the presence of the monarch and consequently of tradition, authority, and security.
7. Gabsaga	One's burial ground	no one knows where he/she will be buried, so it is no use limiting your kindness to people of your own tribe only. You are the child of the world.

Name	Literal Meaning	Literary Meaning
8. Watkuna	I united you	name for a child who is to be a peace-maker or one who would unite his family.
9. Na'vala	Our family is meant for death.	It is like a song of lamentation – a name given to a child after many have died in the family. It is hoped that death will spare this one.
10. Ganse	There is no medicine (against death)	The name indicates that the family requires no medicine for self-protection against death.
11. Lebkuna	I can't leave my brother or sister. I have delivered my brother and sister	If you have a child, that child is your brother or sister, especially if you have none.
12. Ndibmun	One's time	Everyone has his/her own time. There is time for everything, so never be too much in a hurry, lest you miss the target in life
13. Yumunbia	What one sows or plants	Whatever you sow or plant is exactly what you will reap.
14. Boghuma	They have surrounded me	I am surrounded by my enemies or friends, therefore I have to be wary of them; in fact, of the whole world in the final analysis.

CONCLUSION

The objective of this chapter was to trace the origin of Mungaka and then to examine its spread and use as a vehicle with which the Bali Nyonga culture is preserved and propagated. It has clearly been demonstrated in this light, that Mungaka owes its early origins to Bati and Bamum languages principally, but also to a lesser extent to Mubako and other neighbouring languages, not excluding the minor languages of the small groups of people that were annexed into the Bali Nyonga group after the split of the Bali Chamba group on their march southwards to their present settlement. Mungaka has thus been presented as a recently created or forged language, but a natural one all the same. It has equally been demonstrated that it carries an important functional load in North West Province in particular, and in the Republic of Cameroon in general, although it is historically speaking one of the 'youngest' of the languages, at least in the grassland area.

The dynamic characteristic of the language has been elucidated. It exists side by side in certain domains with the original language of the Bali Chamba group, Mubako. Mungaka continues, like many other languages, to grow in all known directions, such as coinage and, above all, linguistic borrowing. The indefatigable, relentless and unflinching role played by the monarchs, amongst other purists, towards the preservation of the purity of Mungaka is evidence of the desperate attempts that men can and are always ready to make to save a cherished language from adulteration or simply from language mixing. But it is known that language is not static, because its users are not either. Contact with people outside the Mungaka speaking community has exposed the language to influences from other languages and cultures. This has had several repercussions on the language, some desirable and others undesirable, since no language will become extinct due to its contact with foreign languages. Mungaka will forever remain a powerful instrument and vehicle of the culture of the Bali Nyonga people.

REFERENCES

Buea Archives. (1973). *Bali Language.* (File No. Ab (1943): 38). Buea Archives.

Chilver, E. M. (1966). *Zintgraff's exploration in Bamenda, Adamawa and the Benue Lands (1889-1892).* Government Printing Press.

Chilver, E. M., & Kaberry, P. M. (1966). *Notes on the pre-colonial history and ethnography of the Bamenda Grassfield* [Unpublished manuscript, privately circulated].

Fokwang, J. K. (1986). *A dictionary of Bali popular names: With a foreword by Dr. Elias M. Nwana* [Mimeographed document, privately circulated].

Greenberg, J. H. (1963). *Languages of Africa*. Mouton & Co.

Guthrie, M., et al. (1956). *Linguistic survey of the northern Bantu borderland* (Vol. 1). O.U.P.

Gwanfogbe, M. B. (1988). Geographical and historical introduction of Bali Nyonga. In *the present volume*.

Koenig, E. L., et al. (1983). *A sociolinguistic profile of urban centers in Cameroon*. Crossroads Press.

Lima, A. S. (1974). *The Mungaka language with special reference to its pronouns* [Unpublished dissertation]. University of Leeds.

Mackey, W. (1972). The description of bilingualism. In J. Fishman (Ed.), *Readings in the sociology of language*. Mouton.

Malcolm, G. (1982). *Through the year in West Africa*. Batsford Academic and Educational Ltd.

Ndangam, A. F. (1972). *Mungaka—A grammatical sketch of its verbal group* [Unpublished dissertation]. University of Leeds.

Ndangam, A. F. (1973). *English loans in Mungaka* [Unpublished dissertation]. University of Leeds.

Ndifontah, B. N. (1988). *The Bali Chamba of Cameroon: A political history*. Editions CAPE.

Nti, D. F. (1973). *A phonological comparison between some aspects of Mungaka (Bali) and English* [Unpublished dissertation]. University of Yaounde.

Nwana, E. M., et al. (1978). *The living culture of Bali Nyonga* [Mimeographed document].

Pike, K. L. (n.d.). *Tone languages*. University of Michigan Press.

Titanji, V. (1988). The traditional political institutions of Bali Nyonga. In *present volume*.

Vielhauer, A. (1944). *Nu a ka n'dze Nku'mu bun Kristo a*. Basel Evangelical Mission.

Suggested Further Reading

Aletum, T. M., et al. (1985). *The traditional political institutions of Bali Nyonga and their contributions to modern politics in Cameroon.* Ministry of Higher Education and Scientific Research, Institute of Human Sciences: Research Centre for Social Sciences, Law and Political Science Department.

Fomuso, S. P. (1985). *Dirges of the Bali Nyonga people (Ntsi vu Ba'ni): A study in folk literature* [Unpublished dissertation]. University of Yaounde.

Gwangwa'a, T., et al. (Eds). (1986). *A publication of the Bali Nyonga students association* [Mimeographed document].

Lima, A. S. (1982). The language of a literary genre in oral literature. *New Horizons: A Journal of Creative and Critical Writing, 2*(2). University of Yaounde (Mimeographed document).

Musi, A. F. (1987). *The Christian missions in Bali: A study of the Basel mission activities 1902-1957* [Unpublished dissertation]. University of Yaounde.

Nusi, J. (1986). *Esquisse phonologique du Ti parler des Ti de la Province de l'Ouest-Cameroun* [Unpublished dissertation]. University of Yaounde.

Pella, F. N. (1984). *Language change and variation: A case study of Mubako* [Unpublished dissertation]. University of Yaounde.

Soh, B. P. (1978). *A study of Bali Nyonga history and the Lela cult* [Mimeographed document].

Vielhauer, A. (1932). *Ndu'ti nwa'ni Ba'ni (Bali primer).* Protestant Missions in the Cameroons.

Vielhauer, A. (1933). *Nwa'ni, kan mfi i Ngan-lunu bo Tita Yesu Kristo ni tsu Ba'ni.* Basel Mission.

Vielhauer, A. (1939). *Ntsi nikob bi ndzobdzob ni tsu Mungaka.* Basel

Evangelical Mission.

Vielhauer, A. (1939). *No'u nku'mu bun Kristo ba evangelisi bi mission ba Basel ma Kamerun.*

6

The Origin of Mungaka
An Alternative View

Gwannua Ndangam

The language widely spoken in Bali Nyonga is Mungaka (Mu = I; nga say; Ka = an emphatic particle). Its lexis and structure are markedly different from the Bali language (Mubako), which is spoken in the other Bali groups of the North West Province.

Very little is known about how Mungaka came to replace Mubako in Bali Nyonga and this remains an interesting area for linguistic research. The language is a dialect of Ba-Ti and there is historical evidence to believe that it developed as a result of contact between the Bali Nyonga group and the Ba-Tis after the break-up of Gawolbe II's army.

In Bali Nyonga, one widely held theory about the origin of the language is that it evolved out of a military necessity. As an army, the Balis wanted a language that was understood by a few so that war plans and strategies could be discussed and kept secret. A language understood by many would easily expose military secrets to speakers of the language.

Thus, Mungaka was used generally and Mubako reserved for making military plans. The flaws in the tacit assumptions here are several. After the split of Gawolbe's army, the factions fought one against the other, e.g., Bali Kumbat and Bali Nyonga fought each other repeatedly. If Bali Nyonga needed to conceal military plans by adopting a language for this, it makes no sense that they would select Mubako, which was spoken by their brothers/ enemies. Besides, the other Chamba groups were warriors, just as Bali Nyonga, and yet we have not witnessed any such arrangement with these other groups

A second theory is that at the time the Bali Nyonga contingent moved into Tsen, after the death of Gawolbe II, the group was predominantly male, spoke mainly Mubako, and had very few women. At Tsen, the Ba-Ti group with whom they came into contact was a female-dominated group speaking Mungaka and with very few men. The different proportions of male to female in the two groups were a perfect situation for the extensive intermarriage which followed. Since children stayed more with their mothers while their fathers were engaged in warfare, the young generation naturally picked up Mungaka, the language spoken by their mothers. More and more generations grew up speaking Mungaka instead of Mubako, and gradually Mungaka speakers increased while Mubako speakers diminished through age and natural death or death at the war front.

This theory seems to give a fairly satisfactory explanation for this linguistic phenomenon. The predominantly male population of the Bali Nyonga group and the predominantly female population of the Ba-Ti group appear to have been a rare coincidence, but the historical events leading up to them are interesting.

During their long journey southwards, women and children moved behind the main army for protection. A "safety gap" was kept in case the men were attacked or if they engaged in fighting. Under Gawolbe II, Prince Mudi was assigned the responsibility of taking care of this special group coming up behind. He was well-known by the women and children, and he presumably knew many of the women by name. When the army broke up into seven factions following the death of Gawolbe II, a majority of the women followed

Mudi, the prince they knew well. The other six groups, including Bali Nyonga, went off with groups made up of mainly men.

The prolonged struggle between the Bamums and the Ba-Tis has already been mentioned in the historical section of this book. The apparently superior forces of the Bamums seemed to have reduced the male population of the Ba-Tis, leaving a community of women — with few men — when the Bali-Nyonga group arrived with a largely male population. Their intermarriage meant that the new generation from this intermarriage was in the hands of Mungaka-speaking women at the stage of first language acquisition. Thus, the development of Mungaka in Bali Nyonga was gradual, as was the "death" of Mubako.

Afterword to the Revised Edition

It is now 37 years since this book was first published in 1988, following the demise of our great Leader HRH VS Galega II in 1985. After the funeral celebrations, I contacted the four co-authors, and we agreed to pay tribute to the great leader by publishing the first edition of the book. In 2016, I once again invited 12 distinguished Bali scholars to produce another book, *Bali Nyonga Today,* which covered not only history, geography, and politics, but also cultural practices and the Bali communities abroad.

Since the publication of the *Introduction to the Study of Bali Nyonga,* several critical studies have been published by other authors, prominent among them, *In Search of Harmony: A History of Bali Nyonga* (Spears Books, 2023) by Dr. Fondi Ndifontah Nyamndi, himself a son of Bali Nyonga and *Lela in Bali: History through Ceremony in Cameroon* by Richard Fardon (Berghahn Books, New York, 2006). These two well-researched works (Nyamndi, 2023; Fardon, 2006) have independently corroborated the central tenets of the narrative presented in our 1988 book. This does not necessarily mean unanimity in every aspect, but rather that an agreement has been reached regarding the facts of the major events described in our book. I will highlight some issues requiring further research and recent developments that have profoundly impacted the culture of Bali Nyonga over the past three to four decades.

HISTORICAL RECORDS

Scholars have not agreed upon the exact nature of the reign of Princess Nahnyonga, the founder of the Bali Nyonga dynasty. They have also not agreed on whether her son, Nyongpasi (Fonyonga I), reached the present site of Bali Nyonga or died earlier somewhere before his son, Galega I, took over from him and established Bali Nyonga at its present site. There is also disagreement about the founder of Balikumbat. According to the oral tradition recorded by us, the founder of Balikumbat was an influential palace retainer of Gawolbe II. Others, however, claim that he was a prince. This latter view is refuted by the fact that in Balikumbat, Voma can be countenanced by women, but not in the other Bali kingdoms, where Voma is countenanced only by men. Another argument is that Balikumbat was not a party to the non-aggression fraternal pact sealed among the split Bali kingdom under the *Jamjam* tree and subsequently did attack Bali Nyonga thrice as it did.

DOUBLE CORONATION AND THE ACCESSION OF GALEGA II TO THE THRONE OF BALI NYONGA

During my research for the book, I met and discussed with two eyewitnesses (Tita Nyagang of Munung Quarter, Mr Wilfred Dook). The difficult transition from Fonyonga II to Galega II characterised by a double coronation in which Tita Nyambi was first installed as king, and several hours later, ousted by a group led by Duga Njingwadnyam Titanji II, after which Galega II was installed. The role that Tita Fokum II (also known as Sama Yenik) played is often glossed over, probably because he was part of the losing team with Tita Nyambi. The genealogy of the Tita Fokum family is not well documented, with some claiming that Tita Fokum I (later succeeded by his sons Sama Yenik Tita Fokum II(A) and Dinga Tita Fokum II(B)) was a servant of Fonyonga II from the Ngie tribe who was later promoted to a place of nobility under Fonyonga II; yet others claim that Tita Fokum I was a descendant of Sub-chief Fongod of the Banten Group. The double coronation is confirmed by Gwanfogbe and Fondi Nyamndi in their works referred to above. At the same time, Gwannua Ndangam gives some details, including the critical role played by Duga Njingwadnyam Titanji II. Future scholars should take up this matter and clarify this chapter of our history, which testifies to the resilience of the Bali community.

GOVERNANCE STRUCTURE AND RELIGION

Lela and Voma are two Institutions that dominated the socioeconomic and cultural calendar of the Bali kingdom until the latter days of Galega II, when their festivals began to be celebrated every other year rather than annually. Subsequently, the festivals of Lela and Voma were not celebrated at all. I recall that the last time Voma was celebrated was in 2015, and the small Lela ceremony took place in 2016. Lela and Voma had religious and military characteristics. Today, Christianity has become the main religion in Bali Nyonga. It has largely replaced Lela and Voma as a religion and has absorbed some melodies of Lela into its liturgy, though with new lyrics. Unless decisive action is taken to restore the Lela and Voma festivals, perhaps with a new management structure and new objectives focused on consolidating cultural identity, brotherhood, and peaceful coexistence, the two emblematic institutions and their festivals may become extinct, and with them a distinctive feature of Bali Nyonga culture.

EVOLUTION OF MUNGAKA, THE LANGUAGE OF BALI NYONGA

Mungaka has evolved significantly since the publication of *An Introduction to the study of Bali Nyonga* in 1988. A new orthography developed for writing African languages has been adapted to replace the Old German orthography. Both scripts are difficult to write and as pointed out by Dr. Beatrice Lima Titanji in *Bali Nyonga Today*, a third orthography using the Latin alphabet and English phonology is being widely used. Furthermore, English and French words have also been integrated into Mungaka, a positive sign that Mungaka may yet survive as Cameroon creates official spaces for indigenous languages within its official French/English bilingualism policy.

URBANISATION AND ENLIGHTENMENT.

Over the past three decades, Bali Nyonga has undergone physical transformation from a rural to a semi-urban area, with asphalt roads replacing earth roads and modern cement-block/zinc-roofed buildings replacing the traditional sundried earth brick houses. The old settlement patterns, with historically ethnic communities living together in one quarter, have been replaced by mixed settlements, especially in new parts of Bali Nyonga, such as Njenka and Wosing. Two new Higher Education Institutions have been established: the Cameroon Christian University (2010) and a Higher Institute in Munung Quarter (2024). New quarters have been established, headed by Quarter Heads (*Tanteh*), who have replaced the sub-chiefs (*Fonte*), whose functions are now ceremonial.

Bali Nyonga is a subdivision with Government administrative services fully installed, replacing traditional governance structures. According to the chieftaincy laws, the Fon or king is now an auxiliary of the central Government with limited powers to arbitrate matters affecting his subjects. The Anglophone crisis has caused significant internal migrations from the centre to villages on the outskirts, such as Mbufung Kubat, Kopin, and Gugong, where new commercial centres are developing.

Though Mungaka remains the main language of communication among the Bali indigenes, English, Pidgin English, and to some extent French are making inroads. It is the collective responsibility of the Bali people to maintain their cultural identity going forward by teaching their language to their children.

Before concluding, let me pay a vibrant homage to my co-authors who have passed on in the meantime: Dr. Elias Nwana, Mr Adolf Sema Lima, and Professor Mathew Basung Gwanfogbe. I acknowledge the prominent participation of the veteran educator and linguist *Ba Nkom* Gwannua Augustine Ndangam, who made significant contributions to the two books mentioned above. He has continued to be active in Bali Nyonga ethnohistory and culture and has produced a reference book entitled *Cultural Encounters* (2014).

I also thank Professor Jude Fokwang for taking up the challenge to republish this book in both hard and electronic copies for wider circulation. He has done an excellent job in writing a new introduction, and I hope this afterword will inspire more scholars to explore Bali Nyonga history and culture as part of the wider effort to deepen understanding of our Cameroonian and African heritage. HRH Galega II was a champion of the modernisation of Bali Nyonga while maintaining its cultural identity. The republication of *An Introduction to the Study of Bali Nyonga is a* timely renewal of the tribute to his rich legacy.

Buea, November 5, 2025
Professor Emeritus Vincent PK Titanji

APPENDIX I

Genealogy of the Bali Nyonga Dynasty

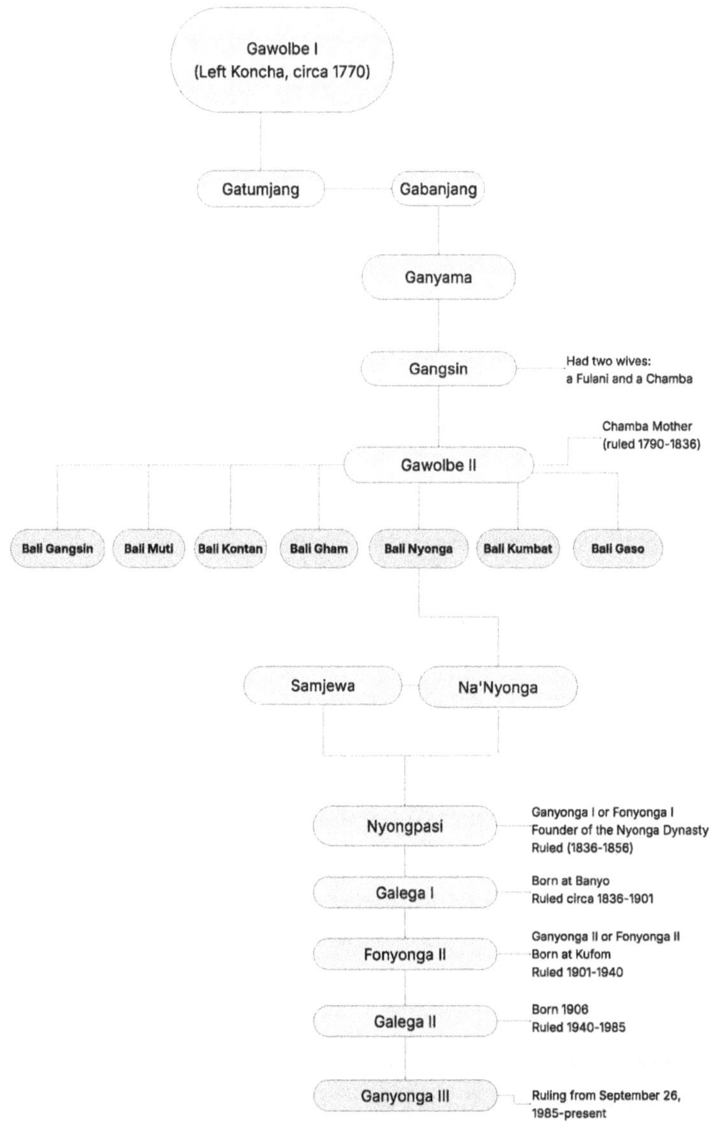

APPENDIX II

An Address By His Highness Ganyonga III
The Fon of Bali on the Occasion of His Presentation to the Bali Population on the 28th September, 1985 at the Fon's Palace, Bali

His Excellency the Governor of the North West Province,
The Senior Divisional Officer, Mezam,
The Subdivisional Officer, Bali,
Hon. Members of Parliament,
Members of Economic Council,
Traditional Dignitaries,

I welcome and salute all of you here on this ceremonial ground during the celebration of the death of our dear father V.S. Galega II, Fon of Bali. I thankfully acknowledge receipt of condolences from all well-wishers and share in the sorrow of my brothers, sisters, mothers and the entire Bali population.

Before my father died, he had willed that I succeed him as your Fon. I have accordingly accepted this responsibility and promise to shoulder it to the best of my ability.

I further wish to express our gratitude to the security and armed forces for their untiring efforts in maintaining peace and harmony in Bali during these difficult times.

On behalf of the Bali people I wish to extend thanks and greetings to the governor of the North West Province, the S.D.O. of Mezam, the D.O. of Bali-Subdivision, Hon. Parliamentarians, Members of Economic Council, Visiting Fons, distinguished guests, all traditional dignitaries, my brothers, sisters, mothers and the entire

Bali population for joining us on the mourning and installation ceremonies,

I appreciate the peace-loving policy of our government and on behalf of the Bali people and my personal self I wish to reaffirm our pledge of loyalty and support to His Excellency President Paul Biya and his government.

I am calling upon all Bali people to continue to actively support the National Party — Cameroon People's Democratic Movement (C.P.D.M.) and to participate in activities of the party as they already have been doing.

LONG LIVE PRESIDENT PAUL BIYA
LONG LIVE THE C.P.D.M.
LONG LIVE THE REPUBLIC OF CAMEROON

APPENDIX III

An Address Presented by The Traditional Council of Bali and the King Makers, on the Occasion of the Presentation of His Royal Highness Dr. Dohsang Ganyonga III After Traditional Installation on the 28th September, 1985, at the Fon's Palace, Bali

His Excellency the Governor of the North West Province,
Senior Divisional Officer,
Subdivisional Office, Bali,
Members of Parliament,
Municipal Administrator, Bali Rural Council,
Members of Economic and Social Council,
Traditional Authorities,
Ladies and Gentlemen,

On this very important occasion, during which the new Fon of Bali is being presented to the Bali population after his installation to the throne of his late father who passed away on the 18/9/85, the Traditional Council and the king makers express their gratitude for your assistance and welcome you all to this solemn ceremony.

Before we continue, we would like to say a few words about his late father. His father was born in Bali Subdivision in 1906. After his primary school career, he decided to take up the Medical Profession and became a Dispensary Attendant in 1924. He served in this capacity for 16 years until 1940, when his father died and he succeeded to the throne on August 30th, 1940

The decade following the Second World War was marked on the continent of Africa by the struggle for Independence. The reign of Fon Galega II is closely bound to this movement for Independence, especially as it relates to Nigeria and Cameroon, and his main contribution is more in political affairs.

He was one of the prominent Cameroonians on the Nigerian political scene between 1950 to 1956 as member of the then Nigerian Eastern House of Assembly and House of Chiefs. In 1956, he represented the West Cameroon natural rulers at the Nigerian Constitutional Conference in London. The West Cameroon Leaders returned from that conference sharply and openly divided over the question of reunification with East Cameroon. Fon Galega II threw his weight irrevocably in favour of secession from Nigeria and reunification with East Cameroon. Subsequently, he campaigned vigorously among the Fons for reunification and through his influence, Bali became one of the main strongholds of the reunification movement under the banner of the K.N.D.P.

After Independence and Reunification came the one other event of considerable weight at the level of the nation; the formation of the national party, the C.N.U., the party leadership in Mezam Division immediately devolved around V.S. Galega II, and he was unanimously elected the first C.N.U. Section President for the Provincial Headquarters in Mezam. But the weight of the responsibility of a traditional monarch was pressing on him and he subsequently accepted to allow another militant to head the Mezam Section of the party during a reorganisation that followed. But he would not abandon the party altogether and was the Sub-Section President for Bali Subdivision until his death.

He was chairman of Bali Council and the one-time sole representative of Southern Cameroons, in the then Eastern Nigeria House of Assembly (1946 to 1950) and also was a member of the then West Cameroon House of Chiefs (1957 to 1972).

His reign has been marked in Bali itself by notable changes and visible developments. On the administrative front, Bali rose from a town to a District and then a Subdivision; a network of unsurfaced roads replaced the narrow lines of footpaths; dark streets in town gave way to electrified ones and closer to the Fon himself, a grass-roofed palace and a cheap traditional mat fence got pulled down and in their places concrete structures, concrete walls and a magnificent grandstand now characterise and modernise the Royal Palace. In agriculture, the farming population rose from subsistence activities to become the main town feeding the teaming population of the Provincial Headquarters. Agricultural economy expanded with the coffee plant becoming the flower in every compound. Behind all these developments, the motivating force was the initiative and effort of His Highness V.S. Galega II.

Typical of natural rulers of his rank and status, he was married to 35 wives and was the father of about 200 children. He lived to see the transformation of the C.N.U. to the C.P.D.M., but the cold hands of death could not permit him to see the functioning of the new C.P.D.M. May his soul rest in peace, in perfect peace.

The new Fon of Bali, His Royal Highness Dr. Dohsang Ganyonga III, son of the late Fon V.S. Galega II, was born on the 25th December 1946. He started his primary School in Bali and completed in Buea Government School in 1958 and had his Secondary Education in Sasse, 1959 to 1963. Thereafter, he worked as a Customs Officer in Limbe, the then Victoria, as well as in the Agricultural Research Department in Ekona as Laboratory Technical Assistant from 1963 to 1967. Still searching for knowledge, he studied Anthropology, Sociology and Psychology at the American University in Cairo, Egypt, from 1969 to 1973 and obtained the Bachelor of Arts Degree with honours. He later on continued his studies in West Germany. He completed his dissertation in 1983, defended the Thesis early in 1984, and was awarded the degree of Doctor of Philosophy (Ph.D.) with honours (Magna Cum Laude).

The traditional Council and the entire population of the Bali people, in this welcoming and installation speech, wish to declare here today their unflinching support and usual loyalty to His Highness Fon Dr. Dohsang Ganyonga III.

Long Live His Royal Highness Dr. Dohsang Ganyonga III, Fon of Bali
Long Live Bali Subdivision
Long Live the Republic of Cameroon.

(Signed)
TITA NJI A.D.
For and on behalf of the Bali Traditional Council and King Makers

Contributors

Prof Mathew B. Gwanfogbe (1943–2024) was a distinguished Cameroonian historian and educator whose career spanned several decades of impactful scholarship and institutional leadership. He served as Vice-Chancellor of the Bamenda University of Science and Technology and previously held the position of Director-Delegate at the Ecole Normale Supérieure (ENS Annex) in Bambili.

A committed contributor to historical research and academic discourse, Dr. Gwanfogbe was the editor-in-chief of the *Pantikar Journal of History*, a founding member of the Cameroon Historical Society, and an active member of the British History of Education Society. His scholarly work focused extensively on the history of education in Cameroon, and his publications remain influential in the field.

Dr. Gwanfogbe was a Knight of the Cameroon Order of Merit and a long-standing member of the Bali Historical Society. He earned his PhD in History from the University of London and was widely respected for his dedication to advancing historical knowledge and educational development in Cameroon.

◆ ◆ ◆

Adolf Sema Lima (1938–2014) was a legendary educationist, humanitarian, and cultural icon from Bali Nyonga, Cameroon. Born on September 23, 1938, to Ba Gwandkuvalla Elias Lima, a renowned educationist, and Na Miriam Papilla, Adolf inherited a passion for learning and service. Named after Basel Missionary Adolf Vielhauer, he embodied the values of his father and the Christian teachings of his community.

Adolf's educational journey began at Native Authority Primary School, Bali (1948–1949), followed by Basel Mission Schools, earning his Standard Six Certificate in 1953. He taught as a Pupil Teacher before obtaining his Teacher's Grade Three (1959) and thereafter, Grade Two Certificates. His linguistic prowess led to teaching roles at Nyasoso Theological College and Kumba's Basel Mission Teachers' Training College. In 1966, he gained admission to the Federal University of Cameroon, Yaoundé, later studying in France, and graduated with a Bilingual Degree in 1970. He earned a Master's from Leeds University in 1975.

A champion of Bali Nyonga culture, Adolf taught Mungaka and promoted its development. He served as a lecturer at the Universities of Yaoundé, Buea, and Cameroon Christian University, shaping countless students. His roles included Deputy Director of Higher Education and GCE Board Moderator in French language and Chief Examiner in English language. Known for generosity and Christian leadership, he was decorated with the Cameroon Knight of the Order of Valour Medal. Married to Alice Yeba Gwanyama, he raised four children and left ten grandchildren. Adolf passed away on July 31, 2014, in Germany, leaving a legacy of education, culture, and faith.

◆ ◆ ◆

Augustine Ndangam (Ba Nkom Gwannua) is a seasoned educator, poet, and cultural advocate whose life's work bridges literature, leadership, and community service. He studied English Language and Literature at the Federal University of Cameroon and the School of English, University of Leeds, United Kingdom, respectively. Between 1979 and 1995, he served in Cameroon's secondary education sector, holding various teaching and administrative positions. He served as Principal of Government High Schools in Wum and Kumbo, and subsequently at Starlight College, Nkwen. He taught at the Higher Teacher's Training College (ENS) Bambili and later at the Bamenda University of Science and Technology as a lecturer. His collaboration with British writer David Weir produced a series of English textbooks that were the leading primary school textbooks in Cameroon for close to three decades.

Ba Ndangam has been a committed community leader and advocate for development in Bali Nyonga. He played a central role in establishing a self-sustaining water system for the community and has supported numerous initiatives to improve the welfare of the Bali people. In recognition of his leadership and service to the community, His Royal Highness V. S. Galega II elevated him to the traditional nobility of Nkom in 1981, conferring upon him the title Nkom Gwannua (the Fon's eyes). He has written extensively on Bali Nyonga culture and language. In tribute to HRH Galega II, Ba Ndangam and four fellow Bali Nyonga scholars co-authored this seminal book on Bali Nyonga culture, history and traditional politics, which was first published in 1988. He is also the author of

Cultural Encounters: Society, Culture and Language in Bali Nyona from the 19th Century, published in 2014.

He is a member of Kadmvi and Sungnyin Ndakums, respectively. He has served as President of Sungnyin and President of the Bali Nyonga Development and Cultural Association (BANDECA) for the Bali Subdivision (2004–2008). In 2004, he delivered the keynote address at the BCA-USA Convention held in Minnesota.

Ba Ndangam is the head of the Ndangam family of Tikali, Bali Nyonga.

◆ ◆ ◆

Prof. Elias Muthias Nwana (1933-2021) was a distinguished Cameroonian scholar, educator, and community leader whose life reflected an enduring commitment to learning, research, and cultural heritage. He pursued higher education at the University of Ghana, Legon, where he earned a degree in Sociology, before continuing to the University of California, Los Angeles (UCLA), where he obtained both Master's and Doctoral degrees in Education. His international academic journey shaped a well-rounded scholar with a deep appreciation for both African and global perspectives on knowledge and development.

Prof. Nwana served Cameroon's secondary and tertiary education sectors with distinction, holding several leadership and academic positions, including Principal of CCAST Bambili, Director of Studies at the Ministry of National Education, Associate Professor at the Higher Teacher Training College (ENS) Bambili, and Vice-Chancellor of the Bamenda University of Science and Technology. In each of these roles, he demonstrated visionary leadership, scholarly excellence, and a steadfast dedication to national educational growth.

Rooted in his native Bali Nyonga, Prof. Nwana was also an accomplished anthropologist and sociologist who curated and interpreted the cultures of the Grassfields region. His research, writings, and mentorship reflected his belief that education and culture are the twin foundations of personal fulfilment, community progress, and national development.

◆ ◆ ◆

Professor Vincent P.K. Titanji, is a Biologist-Biochemist who earned his PhD degree in Physiological Chemistry from Uppsala University in Sweden (1978) following a Master's degree in Animal Biochemistry from the Lomonosov Moscow State University (1973). He currently serves as Vice Chancellor of the Metropolitan University Institute and Emeritus Professor & Honorary Dean at the Faculty of Science, University of Buea.

Previously, he served as Vice Chair of the African Union's Scientific Research and Innovation Council (ASRIC-AU). He also served as the Vice-Chancellor & CEO of the Cameroon Christian University Institute (2015- 2020); Vice President of the African Academy of Sciences for the Central African Region (2014-2020);TWAS Visiting Professor of Biotechnology at Addis Ababa University (2015-2019); Rector/Vice-Chancellor (2006-2012) of the University of Buea (UB); Pioneer Dean (1993-1998) of UB Faculty of Science; Founding Coordinator/Director (1986- 1997) of the Biotechnology Centre, Nkolbisson, at the University of Yaoundé 1, Cameroon; Founding Coordinator (1994-2012) of the Biotechnology Unit, University of

Buea; President (2000-2009) of the Federation of African Societies of Molecular Biology and Biochemistry (FASBMB); Board Chair (2007-2010) of the Biosciences Eastern and Central African Network (Be CA); Board member of the International Council for Science Regional Office for Africa (ICSU –ROA 2005-2010).

Professor Titanji has received several awards including: The International Society of Infectious Diseases (ISID) Prize, New York award for The African W.H.O. region in 1992; The International Foundation for Science/Danish International Development Agency's Prize (IFS) DANIDA for noteworthy contributions to science in 1998, the The Cameroon Knight of the Order of Valor in 2003 & 2010, The CAS distinguished Services Award in 2022.

Professor Titanji is married to Dr. Beatrice Lebsia Kahboh Titanji nee Lima and they have four children.

Index

www.ingramcontent.com/pod-product-compliance
Lightning Source LLC
Chambersburg PA
CBHW030314270326
41926CB00010B/1362
* 9 7 8 1 9 5 7 2 9 6 6 9 2 *